The Church among Deaf People

14KD6

Church House Publishing,
Church House,
Great Smith Street,
London SW1P 3NZ

ISBN 0 7151 3803 0

Published 1997 for the Advisory Board of Ministry of the General Synod
by Church House Publishing

Cover design by Julian Smith. The front cover photograph shows Davina
Merricks signing 'Deaf Church'.

Printed in England by The Cromwell Press Ltd, Melksham, Wiltshire.

GS 1247

The Church among Deaf People

A Report prepared by a Working Party
of the Committee for Ministry among Deaf People
for the General Synod of the Church of England's
Advisory Board of Ministry

Advisory Board of Ministry
Ministry Paper No. 14

CHURCH HOUSE PUBLISHING

Contents

Members of the Working Party

The following served as members of the Working Party:

The Revd Vera Hunt	Chairman
	Chaplain among Deaf People, London Diocese
The Revd Gill Behenna	Chaplain among Deaf People, Exeter Diocese
The Revd Canon James Clarke	Joint Secretary, Committee for Ministry among Deaf People
Mrs Sarah James	Vice-Chairman, Committee for Ministry among Deaf People
	Vice-Chairman, Central Readers Council
	Member of General Synod
The Revd Mike Sabell	Chaplain among Deaf People, Lichfield Diocese
The Revd Canon Frank Tanner	Chaplain among Deaf People, Peterborough Diocese
The Revd Gaynor Turner	Ordinand, Manchester Diocese
Secretary:	
The Revd Douglas Caffyn	Joint Secretary, Committee for Ministry among Deaf People
	Chaplain among Deaf People, Chichester Diocese

Terms of Reference

To report on the present state of the Church among Deaf People within the Church of England and to make recommendations.

> Quotations within boxes are comments made by deaf people during interviews with members of the Committee.

Foreword

Since the Committee for Ministry among Deaf People became part of the Advisory Board of Ministry, we have valued even more the contribution that deaf people can and do make to the life of the Church.

This Report is intended to spread the good news about the place of deaf people in the Church, and to deepen understanding of their gifts and needs. I warmly welcome it as a valuable part of the material that is available through ABM, and I believe that it will enable many more people to understand and support this aspect of ABM's work.

✠ John Hereford

Chairman

Advisory Board of Ministry

Preface

The Church of England has a long and honourable tradition in its work with deaf people. Many of the centres and other services for deaf people had their origins in its work of care and concern.

In recent years many dioceses have had to recognise that Ministry among Deaf People is now their concern, rather than it being left to voluntary society provision. One major benefit of this change is that deaf congregations and the chaplains are more than ever seen as part of the whole life of the Church, central to its concerns. It is now normal to see a deaf group at all major diocesan events, sharing fully in them, and contributing to the liturgies and life of the Church in this and other ways.

We have prepared this book in order to provide information for those who may come into contact with deaf people, or have to make decisions about the provision of resources for this very specialised ministry. When the spending of every pound has to be weighed carefully, it is vital that information is available in accessible and understandable form. We believe this book will help in the making of decisions, by giving a clear statement of the needs and opportunities in this most exciting and challenging area of the Church's work.

I am delighted to commend it to you.

✠ John Chelmsford

Chairman

Committee for Ministry among Deaf People

Acknowledgements

The Committee for Ministry among Deaf People would like to thank the following deaf people who came to Church House, Westminster to be interviewed about their knowledge of the Church among Deaf People:

Jennifer Aldridge

Ken Dyson

Trevor Landell

Bill Palmer

Arnold Rundle

Bob Shrine

Edith Tabrar

Len Tabrar

Jenny Weir

We would also like to thank Miss Margaret Moore and Mrs Pam Gallagher for their advice on Chapter 7. We would also like to express our gratitude to the Revd Ros Hunt and the Revd Philip Maddock for their comments on the Church among Deaf People and for interpreting at our meetings.

CHAPTER 1

One faith, one Church, one Lord

> 'When I worship in a hearing church, they seem to have a different God from mine.'
>
> 'Deaf people ask the same questions as hearing people; questions like: why are there wars and suffering?'
>
> 'We can share times of prayer, hearing and deaf people. We are one community when we pray together.'
>
> 'When I am in a hearing Church, I feel as if I am an ornament. When I am in a deaf Church, I feel really part of it.'

1.1   We possess one faith, we are members of one Church, we worship one Lord, yet normally deaf and hearing people worship separately. This book sets out the reasons, considers some of the implications and makes recommendation for the future.

1.2   The Article of Religion XXIV states under the heading 'Of speaking in the congregation in such a tongue as the people understandeth.'

> It is a thing plainly repugnant to the Word of God, and the custom of the Primitive Church to have public prayer in the Church, or to minister the Sacraments, in a tongue not understood of the people.

The language of deaf people is sign language. Many deaf people cannot understand speech.

1.3   When a person is baptised and welcomed into the Church, the following statement is made by the congregation:

> We welcome you into the Lord's family. We are members together of the body of Christ; we are children of the same

1

heavenly Father; we are inheritors together of the kingdom of God. We welcome you.

When in a family the different members do not speak to each other, we recognise that evil has overcome good. Is not the same true when there is no communication between the hearing and deaf members of the family of the Church?

1.4   In order for members of the deaf community to feel welcome within the family of the whole Church their language, sign language, should be used.

1.5   Suppose for one moment that all Church services were to be conducted in a purely visual medium; no sound, no voice, no music allowed. We would think that very odd indeed. We would think the experience incomplete. Information would be missing and people who were partially sighted would be discriminated against. For deaf people, services which rely heavily on spoken words are incomplete experiences.

1.6   If ministers go overseas to a foreign country, first they learn the language and the culture of the people where they will serve, then they start their work. Equally, ministers who come to the deaf community need to learn the language and culture of deaf people before they start work. Only then can ministry to deaf people adequately be carried out.

1.7   Many deaf people remember clearly the experience of sitting in Church services, unable to hear or understand what was happening. It is often difficult for these same people to feel accepted as adult disciples.

1.8   'Ephphatha' Be opened! The healing of the deaf man is a beautiful example of the love and compassion of Jesus for deaf people. He took the deaf man aside, put his fingers in his ears, spat, and touched his tongue. Jesus was communicating with the deaf man by means of symbolic gestures. The deaf man then heard the words of Jesus. The Church must do all it can to ensure that people who are deaf can hear the words of Jesus now. Just as Jesus took the deaf man aside to heal him, so now separate provision needs to be made for deaf people within the family of the one Church.

2

1.9   Yet there will always be a tension between the disunity caused by different modes of communication and the maintenance of the spiritual communion of the whole of the Church. Where there is integrated worship this problem may not be so obvious. But there are still few parishes, deaneries or dioceses who ensure that the deaf community is included in their activities, festivals, quiet days, teaching, ordinations and missions. At all of these, deaf people should have the opportunity to be present and to take part. Normally this means that trained, qualified interpreters will be needed.

1.10   It is important that all Christians work together. Within most deaf Christian communities there are people who come from different religious traditions and all are accepted equally. Denominational differences between the Anglican and Free Churches have not been carried over into the deaf community, and in some dioceses the Roman Catholics join in the diocesan chaplains meetings. At conferences Roman Catholic priests and lay people come to share their experiences and understanding.

1.11   At the international level the International Ecumenical Working Group provides a forum for sharing our growing understanding of ministry by and among deaf people. There is a bi-annual meeting attended by representatives from 25 countries. Links with other Anglican deaf communities are steadily being developed. It is ironic that, while great progress has been made in co-operation internationally and ecumenically in the Church of England as a whole, deaf members of the Church often feel neglected and marginalised by their Christian brothers and sisters.

1.12   St Paul sums it up in I Corinthians 12:

> If the ear should say, 'Because I am not an eye, I do not belong to the body,' that would not make it any less a part of the body. If the whole body were an eye, where would be the hearing? ... God arranged the organs in the body, each one of them as he chose. ... The parts of the body which seem to be weaker are indispensable. ... If one member suffers, all suffer together; if one member is honoured, *all rejoice together.* (RSV)

3

CHAPTER 2

A deaf person: An individual and in community

> 'Captioned TV, text telephones, the demise of residential schools as well as videos and fax machines have brought deaf people into a larger world. At the same time they have eroded the traditional places where deaf people gathered and sign language stories were shared.'

2.1   To hear is as natural and effortless an occurrence as it is invisible. Man would as soon ask himself how breathing keeps him physically alive as how hearing keeps him psychologically alive. He simply does not think of it at all.

(Levine, 1960: p. 17)

2.2   In order to grasp the implications of deafness, it is first necessary to recognise the function of hearing and its place in human life and communication.

2.3   Hearing provides constant, uninterrupted information about the environment all around the person; it does not have to be focused, nor does it stop when something is out of sight, nor even stop totally when the person is asleep. Hearing thereby provides information that tells the person whether they are safe, in familiar surroundings, and when disturbance is about to happen. It gives warning of somebody coming, and a series of signals, door bells, alarm clocks, timing signals, and so on, indicate that something is about to happen or has happened.

2.4   Hearing also keeps people in touch with one another; in a household a mother can leave a child in one room, knowing that the child's cries will alert her, and the child will be aware of her presence. The regular

4

activities of daily life make sounds that tell members of the household, a business, school or any kind of community, that others are present and doing various things. The most vital contribution this makes is a sense of personal security and belonging, and a view of self as part of a community or group.

2.5   Hearing also provides the means for most direct interpersonal communication – speaking and listening. Language is carried on the sounds of words, uttered and received. Out of this grow relationships, education, entertainment and many other facets of human life. The essential nature of the telephone is its ability to convey speech from one to another, and the difficulty of life without it serves to illustrate how important is talking to one another.

2.6   Hearing contributes greatly to the learning of language itself. Speech develops from hearing others speak and from attempts to copy what is heard; much of this is not deliberate, not taught, but is part of the massive learning of the early years.

2.7   Hearing is also an enormous source of information, of acquisition of facts and opinions, of beliefs and prejudices, of knowledge and understanding, of attitudes and of views from within communities and families. There is a constant bombardment of information from the radio and TV, and the availability of verbal information through the audio pathway is almost as unavoidable as the availability of sound information from the environment.

2.8   Deafness is the absence of all or some part of hearing. An awareness of what hearing contributes to the life of an individual shows how profound the impact of that loss can be:

> Most of us live in a world of sounds. We are surrounded by all kinds of sounds. Often we take them for granted. We give them little thought until we unexpectedly do not hear them. Nevertheless, we thoroughly depend on sounds to get through our everyday lives. We would be lost without them.

> (Higgins, 1980: p. 21)

5

2.9   It is easier to describe what a deaf person is not, than what a deaf person is. For example, a deaf person is not a hearing person who cannot hear; a deaf person is not someone who lives in a world of total silence; a deaf person is not someone who hears nothing, and deaf people are no more the same as each other as are hearing people.

2.10   The effect of deafness on the individual varies according to many factors, chief among them being not the degree of deafness, but when deafness began. Deafness of ageing, and deafness occurring in adult life are both serious matters, and require attention and special careful treatment (and ministry) but they are very different in effect from deafness which occurs at or before birth, or in early infancy. Deafness which starts in adult life is considered in Chapter 8.

2.11   The major difference relates to communication – deafness which occurs in adult life certainly disrupts communication, but it does not affect the language in which a person communicates, especially in expressive communication (what is said or transmitted). This will remain English, and access to the written word will remain the same. Deafness occurring in early life, however, makes all means of communication visual, and the development of spoken English is radically affected. The outcome is that the natural language for such deaf people will be visual, transmitted by signs and gestures, which is called 'Sign Language'. It is the language of the deaf community, which defines itself by the fact that it is culturally identified by the use of sign language within its activities.

2.12   A further consequence of this radical change affects thinking; rational thinking in a hearing person is dominated by verbal images, so it follows that if a person is not able to hear or imagine the sounds of words, and operates in a visual language format, then thinking must also be in that visual format.

2.13   Because there is not so much information available in appropriate visual means as there is in sound for a hearing person, there will be a serious shortage of vocabulary, and of knowledge that flows from overheard as well as taught input. Deaf people may not be as familiar with written English as their hearing peers and attempts to write in English may prove very difficult for some of them.

2.14   These differences mean that a deaf person is faced with even more difficulties than a hearing person when presented with English texts, prayer books, the Alternative Service Book, or the Bible, and will find worship presented wholly in spoken language, sung or said, and relying on the set texts of the Church of England, an alien medium.

2.15   Another consequence of lack of exposure to spoken English is that, unless a deaf person has been brought up in a totally visually orientated family, with fluent use of sign language from a very early age, he or she is likely to be unfamiliar with many of the everyday facts that are taken for granted, will have much less access to written English than comparable hearing peers, and will have gaps in knowledge, both general and specific (e.g. religious knowledge) that demand special attention in ministry.

2.16   As well as the effect on communication, early profound deafness will radically change an individual's relationship with the world – there will be much less direct contact with the surroundings. Vision is a focused sense, and only operates where a person is looking, and when awake with eyes open. Therefore, relationships with parents, children and others in a household, for example, will be less and different.

2.17   A consequence of this may be a loss of personal security and weaker bonds of contact between people. Once a deaf person looks away, or goes out of sight of another person, contact is almost totally lost. There are implications for ministry in this change, and in the need to recognise other possible changes, for example, in self-perception and feelings of wholeness. On the other hand, many deaf people are much more visually aware than their hearing peers. Their skills of concentration and retention are very well developed. All trainee teachers are told: 'What is heard is forgotten, what is seen is remembered, what is done is understood.' Deaf people are good at remembering and seem to be able to make better pictures in their minds. They often see things around them more clearly and see things in their minds more clearly.

7

2.18   Deaf people often make better use of the information which they receive than many hearing people would. A hearing child of deaf parents wrote: 'When I was a boy, my father, who was profoundly deaf, always seemed to know when I was doing something naughty, as if he had eyes in the back of his head.' Deaf parents are perfectly capable of caring for babies even though they cannot hear their crying.

2.19   Deafness is a condition that affects the outsider as well as the person who is deaf. If hearing people want to contact or communicate with a deaf person, then they have to change their behaviour, they have to be visually accessible, at the very least they need to speak directly and clearly.

2.20   On a wider scale, for a deaf person to have free access to the opportunities of society, special arrangements have to be made with visual information and people who can sign at key points. Failure to provide these things in the past has meant that many deaf people have grown up feeling that they are discriminated against, and that they are second-class citizens. Among the present generation of deaf leaders, ideas like 'identity' and 'struggle' feature prominently, and there are those who feel that the Church should adopt a liberation stance in its dealing with, and on behalf of, deaf people.

2.21   All these things mean that deafness is likely to affect the faith of the individual and of the community, and the way in which it is acquired.

2.22   Traditionally, deaf individuals belonged to deaf community groups, which were largely based around social welfare centres for deaf people, often called 'Missions', and originating in the early nineteenth-century church activity, trying to 'take the Gospel to those who could not hear it'.

2.23   In these centres, deaf people made friends, relaxed, and enjoyed themselves in the company of other deaf people, able to use a common language, free to sign to each other without having to struggle with the language of the hearing world in which they lived.

2.24 In most of them there was a full programme of events, and recreational activity, in which church and worship took a significant part. The organisation was often led by a Reader or designated minister of the Church of England. At one time, the 'Missioner' would act as worship leader, interpreter, welfare officer, community organiser, and even chairman of the Deaf Social Club.

2.25 For this group of people the deaf community was very important, and friendships made at school were still alive late into life; it was the focus of much of their lives, and the decline of their clubs in recent years has been a source of grief to many elderly deaf people.

2.26 The deaf community changed over a period from the mid-1960s onwards, as changes in technology and education took effect. Text telephones made the arrangement of meetings possible without physically attending the deaf centre, and text subtitling and signed programmes on TV have made entertainment at home more possible. The changes which took social welfare provision away from the deaf centres and into local authority and specialist units, the introduction of Interpreter Services, the growth of a better educated deaf elite, and the generally more positive attitude of society towards deaf people, have all contributed to a very deep change in attitudes within deaf communities themselves.

2.27 Now it is recognised that the 'deaf community' is not homogeneous, not one fixed group of people; it is continually changing, and deaf people opt in and out according to their desires or attitudes. It is above all an elective community, to which deaf people may choose to belong.

2.28 Present experience of deaf community life shows that it is now the base for much political as well as recreational and artistic activity, a platform for calling for change in social provision, and for challenging for legal and civil rights for deaf people (e.g. lobbying for a Disabled Rights Bill and asking for recognition by the Church).

2.29 Modern deaf communities expect deaf leadership, and call for it in all parts of life that affect them. This has implications for the Church, and its provision of ministry and worship opportunities for deaf people.

2.30   Deaf communities have their own particular strengths: there is little class distinction; in a group of deaf people the signing is very public and everyone can see what is being said so communication is very open. Visual language and facial expressions are informative, sometimes dramatic. Great attention is paid to the speaker; each person is given time to speak and others do not interrupt.

2.31   Because someone is profoundly deaf, it does not mean that they are automatically members of the deaf community. Being deaf gives them the right to be members, in the sociological and psychological sense, but does not mean they are members, which is a matter of choice. For some this is a serious loss, as less adequate, less well-educated, less competent deaf people are in danger of being left out and alone in a society which is still an alien and hostile environment. It is appropriate for the Church to bring deaf people together, in order to enable them to find a community and social base for their individual lives. In this way, drawing deaf people together becomes an act of pastoral care in itself, as well as an opportunity for evangelism and worship.

2.32   Changes in the nature and status of deaf communities also mean that there are many more places where deaf people can meet, specific pubs and clubs are the focus of certain groups of deaf people with special identities or cultures, and other places are just casual meeting points for deaf people of certain ages and interests. It is necessary for a minister among deaf people to be ready to seek out these places, and attend them from time to time to make contact. That contact will need to be sensitive, because a community's relationship with a chaplain, deaf or hearing, is one that will have to be determined, and the right of access earned, on the basis of the chaplain's respect for, and acknowledgements of, the community's identity, culture and language.

CHAPTER 3

The Church's involvement
with deaf people

> *'I pray with my eyes open, not shut like hearing people. God comes through my heart, shares my thoughts. When I was confirmed I thought it was a new way of living my life; I was frightened but God showed me the way and he showed me how I should live. Now I have responsibility to show people the way, Christ's way.'*

3.1   In 1576 a deaf couple were married in St Martin's Church, Leicester. Sign language was used and a ritual was devised that made it clear that the couple understood what they were doing, and that the marriage was entirely legal in the eyes of the law and the Church.

3.2   In the 1890s, an organisation was begun, in the vestry of the same church in Leicester, which eventually became a diocesan-wide organisation for the spiritual, emotional, educational and physical welfare of deaf people. Its early impetus was twofold, to remove poverty from a particular group, and to enable them to 'hear' the Gospel for the first time.

3.3   At the same time, a group of deaf people, led by a deeply religious deaf man, came together determined to maintain the faith they had learned in their residential school in Derby. These two movements met, and led to the foundation of what became the 'Leicester and County Mission for the Deaf' (now the Leicester Centre for Deaf People) and the establishment of such a strong Church among Deaf People, that when a fine new Centre was built in 1960, a 100-seater church was integral to it, and placed at the very heart of the building.

3.4   In his book, *A Tower of Strength*, published in 1992, Patrick Beaver tells us that in 1841 some former pupils of the London Asylum 'finding that neither State nor Church had made any provision for them', agreed to meet together every Sunday in a room in Fetter Lane, London, for prayer and worship. This little 'Church' grew, until its activities eventually came to the notice of some wealthy hearing people who came to support it. Then, led by a clergyman, the Reverend Sam Smith, who had been a teacher at the Doncaster Institution for the Deaf, these people collected funds for the building of St Saviour's, Oxford Street, the first church for the deaf. The Church and Social Centre was opened in 1873 by Queen Victoria who then conferred royal patronage on the movement – The Royal Association in Aid of the Deaf and Dumb – later The Royal Association in aid of Deaf People (RAD), which was the agency in the UK to promote the spiritual welfare of the deaf. Queen Alexandra, herself deaf, was a frequent visitor to St Saviour's, where she could enjoy the company of other people and, being a fluent finger-speller, was able to follow the services. It is probable that Alexandra was taught British finger-spelling by Queen Victoria herself, for the Queen had become fluent in it in her younger days. St Saviour's Church moved to Acton in 1924.

3.5   Similar stories can be told about many towns in this country. The Victorian outreach to the poor and deprived in society was touched by the obvious needs and deprivation of deaf people, and the newly educated deaf school-leavers (it became a right for deaf children only in 1897) wanted to express themselves in faith and life with other deaf people.

3.6   The Church in England, especially the Church of England (it is replicated in Scotland by the Church of Scotland), can take credit for the foundation of many organisations which care for the profoundly deaf people in their midst, and for the development of primitive social welfare services among them. Before the start of the Second World War these services had become more wide-ranging and sophisticated, although depending on the overworked and underpaid Missioners, who were quite often the children of deaf parents, or deaf themselves. They worked all hours, and did all tasks, including religious education and the leading of services, as well as interpreting in any situation that called for it.

3.7   The Church can also take credit that through these organisations, and the church services they offered, sign language was kept alive and at a high level through many years when much educational theory tried to deny it, and actively prevented children from using it in education, and tried to prevent its use in their homes. Within the 'Missions', deaf centres and churches, sign language was the common language and was encouraged and used by nearly all who attended.

3.8   Gradually over the years, society as a whole, and the Church in particular (often in the vanguard), have become more aware of the obligation to enable people with any kind of handicap or dependence to lead as full a life as possible. It is now commonplace, for example, for local authorities to provide wheelchair access to essential and recreational facilities, and for tourist attractions to cater for blind people. The development in general sensitivity towards people who have in the past been marginalised is likely to continue. Appreciation of the gifts people bring and adequate provision for their needs are essential for a civilised society.

3.9   Since the Second World War, as the state in various ways has accepted more responsibility for meeting the needs of deaf people, the deaf centres have changed and declined in importance, and the total reliance on voluntary and church income has ceased. Now, because only a very small number of chaplains are employed by voluntary organisations, it is the responsibility of the Church to provide Ministry among Deaf People. The pattern today, and for the future, is that deaf people will be served by ministers employed by the Church. These ministers will be either deaf themselves or be trained in the use of sign language and be knowledgeable about the effects of deafness and the impact it has on people's lives.

3.10   In 1927 the General Assembly of the Church of England set up the Council for the Deaf which, together with its successors, encouraged and advised dioceses and individuals in this work. The present Committee for Ministry among Deaf People has the responsibility (to the Advisory Board of Ministry):

'to encourage and strengthen the participation of deaf people in the life and witness of the Church, to represent the views of deaf people to the Church and of the Church to deaf people, and to support the work of their chaplains.'

Chapter 4

Worship

The service begins at 3.00 p.m., but already by 2.15 p.m. there are several people standing in silence outside the church door waiting for the caretaker: they are wearing gloves against the bitter cold but their fingers are busy as they tell each other the news of the past month. Half an hour later they are part of a congregation of thirty, greeting everyone, still in silence; communicating by sign it's as easy to talk to someone across the chapel as to the person sitting beside you.

The service follows the pattern of Rite A but at a different pace; the hymns are led by the deaf choir and signed to the rhythm of the signs rather than the rhythm of the traditional tunes; the responses are led by a person standing on the opposite side of the chapel from the presiding minister; for the intercessions each person comes forward to light a candle and signs 'I light this candle for ...', so the whole community can share each person's concerns as they are brought before God.

Every service is different. Sign language cannot be written in a book and so there is no fixed text. The bible readings are told afresh at every service. The prayers are recreated. Because all the information is visual, the congregation concentrate on every word. In the service there is plenty of time and every action is deliberate and dignified; the devotion is profound. After the service everyone goes to the hall for tea and then the 'talking' really begins; for some people this may be one of the only two or three times in the month when they will talk to people who can really understand them.

Even after the doors are locked they seek the light of a street lamp and continue talking until finally the cold starts to eat into the bones and everyone goes home.

Where and how

4.1   In most dioceses deaf people gather together for regular worship. Approximately 10 per cent of these services are held weekly, 20 per cent fortnightly, 60 per cent monthly and 10 per cent quarterly.

4.2   Those who attend services for deaf people are profoundly deaf people who use sign language, hearing children of deaf people, hearing and deaf professionals working with deaf people, and hearing people who are learning sign language.

4.3   The Church of England regularly holds services for deaf people in 135 places, of these, 111 are services held specifically for deaf people and 24 are services where the majority of the congregation are hearing people.

4.4   Statistics of those who attend services are always difficult to collect but about 1,700 deaf people attend regular services. In addition, about 450 hearing people attend the services held specifically for deaf people. The average congregation includes about twelve deaf people. We know of eleven congregations which have more than 25 deaf people as members and no regular congregation of more than 50. However, the congregations at festival services are often a hundred or more.

Venues

4.5   Because many of the deaf missions were originally founded by Christian organisations there is a tradition for one room in the deaf centre being set apart as a chapel specially designed to suit the needs of the deaf people. About 60 per cent of the services for deaf people are held in deaf centres or in Social Services premises where deaf clubs meet. The other services are held in local parish churches, 25 per cent being specifically for deaf people and the remaining 15 per cent jointly with hearing congregations.

4.6   A chapel which has been designed and furnished with deaf people's needs in mind will have the following features:

(a) Good lighting – deaf people rely on visual information, so they need to be able to see well.

(b) Clear sight lines from the congregation to the 'action of the service'. This may include the use of raised seating.

(c) Plain backgrounds against which to sign, and plain robes and vestments for the ministers.

(d) Strong visual images – symbols, colours, pictures, icons, which give information and set the mood in the absence of music.

(e) Provision and storage of visual aids (OHP, screen, flip chart).

(f) Facilities for providing tea and a space to talk before and after the service.

4.7 In many chapels the furnishings have been made by deaf people themselves, (carpentry being one of the traditional trades of deaf people). This gives a very strong link with the history of the deaf community.

4.8 One place of worship may well serve a third or more of a diocese. Many of the congregation are dependent on public transport which on a Sunday is often inadequate or non-existent. It is important that the places of worship are as easily accessible as possible and that people recognise the transport problems which for deaf people are inevitable, but which many hearing Christians would find unacceptable.

Liturgy

4.9 At 70 per cent of those places where the Church of England regularly holds services for deaf people all services are the Eucharist, at 20 per cent there is both Eucharistic and non-Eucharistic worship, and at 10 per cent all worship is non-Eucharistic.

4.10 All the information and all the cues in the service are visual not auditory (as in a service for hearing people). The hymns, prayers and responses which are signed by all the congregation are led by a minister at the front of the church who sets the speed so that everyone can keep together. Deaf people cannot listen to their neighbour. No-one can hear the door open and shut as people enter, coughing, the turning of the pages of the service book or a person singing out of tune. So care needs to be taken to ensure a sense of community during the service, for example by sitting in a circle and by sharing the peace. The pace of the service is different. The delay between versicles and responses is slightly longer than in a spoken or sung service as the congregation need to change their eye gaze from one minister to the other. Similarly, songs and hymns when signed without music have a different pace and rhythm from the sung versions.

4.11   Hearing people, in most places, have a choice of different styles of liturgy available to them, e.g. High Mass, said Eucharist, Morning Prayer, Evening Prayer. The same choice is not available to deaf people who often have to travel 10 or 20 miles to find a service at all. So most ministers consider it right to maintain a relatively middle-of-the-road-style of worship. There are, as yet, no rock services, but there is considerable diversity. In some churches the sermon is interactive because deaf people are much more willing to participate than hearing people. In some places the planning and leading of the services are a community activity, at others the minister plans and conducts the whole service.

4.12   One special element of many services is a deaf choir. The hymns are signed in unison by a group of men and women often wearing robes. Individual words or phrases of the hymn are signed using standard sign language but linking them with a rhythm and pattern which is expressive and beautiful. In preparing these hymns there is always discussion about the meaning of the words and the overall meaning of the hymn. Often this becomes a 'hymn and bible study' for all the choir members. It is important that every person can see the choir or the leader of the hymn, so deaf worshippers do not normally stand up for hymns but remain seated.

4.13   Some deaf people can appreciate music, as is clear to anyone visiting a disco for deaf people. Rhythm and pace are important features of sign language and at some services hymns and songs are accompanied by a piano or keyboard. However, in deaf worship music is of secondary importance and many deaf congregations never use it.

4.14   In some churches for hearing people there have been great developments in the use of such visual features in worship as film, videos or changing colours, but most chaplains among deaf people have had neither the time nor resources to exploit these opportunities to the full.

Language

(See Glossary on p.65 for a full explanation of the terms used.)

4.15   The mode of communication in the services depends on the needs of the people and the ability of the ministers. The service may be in British Sign Language (BSL) or Sign Supported English (SSE) and there may or may not be a voiced interpretation given. Sometimes a sign language interpreter may be used to interpret for a hearing person who cannot sign. In some services different modes will be used for the different sections, for example, BSL for stories and the sermon, and SSE for the liturgical text.

4.16   An oral approach to education has suppressed BSL, the language of deaf people, over the last one hundred years. The Church has not supported this, but has continued to offer services in sign language. Education is now changing rapidly and in many places deaf children are being taught in sign language. However, many older deaf people have been taught that if sign language is to be used, especially in a formal setting, it should be SSE.

4.17   Many deaf people are becoming aware of the validity of BSL, which as a language has moved from being something used only in informal situations, to being the language of conferences and the theatre. BSL poets and actors are demonstrating the beauty of it as a visual language. Within the deaf community there is a small, but persistent, cry for Church services in BSL. Some younger deaf people give the continued use of SSE as their reason for not attending Church services. Older deaf people continue to insist that it is the only proper language for a formal service. Chaplains live with this tension and are continually trying to update and improve their communication skills.

4.18   BSL has a beauty and grace just as much as any spoken language. This is another element which can help in worship but cannot be recorded and replicated. The ministers need to recreate this beauty in every service.

Integrated and interpreted services

4.19   Some churches offer integrated services for deaf and hearing people. These vary in quality from being fully integrated to simply providing a sign language interpreter for a normal service for hearing people.

4.20   In a truly integrated service, deaf and hearing people worship together with an equal balance of their languages and cultures. A great deal of careful thought, planning, and consultation needs to take place in order to make such services successful. For example, some bible passages cannot be signed at the same speed as they are normally read: one of the Christmas Day readings, Luke 2. 1–14, includes in the first four verses the words: Caesar Augustus, Quirinius, Syria, Joseph, Galilee, Nazareth, Judaea, David and Bethlehem; each of these proper nouns needs to be finger-spelt letter by letter in sign language.

4.21   In an integrated service the interpreters must not only be well qualified as interpreters but also have a good understanding of theology and liturgy. They need to be well briefed and have printed copies of all of the service including the sermon several days beforehand, so that they can have adequate time to prepare. It is essential that a fair balance is kept between spoken language which is interpreted into sign for deaf people, and sign language which is interpreted into speech for hearing people.

4.22   The advantage of an integrated service is that deaf people are able to worship in a much larger gathering and so avoid the possibility of isolation which exists for many of the small congregations worshipping separately.

4.23   If the regular diet of worship is only interpreted services, with a sign language interpreter transmitting solely to deaf people what is being said and sung, then for everyone the worship is incomplete. Deaf people should be enabled to lead parts of the worship and appropriate voice-over interpretation should be provided for non-signing people.

4.24   Some individual deaf people choose to worship in the company of hearing people, others have no alternative place for communal worship. Proper provision should be made according to the resources available. For example, there should be a clear view of the minister from where they sit, hymn numbers should be easily seen, and if they are accompanied by an interpreter, then the interpreter needs to sit facing the congregation.

> *'In a hearing church there are too many words. A deaf church is less boring; there is more interaction during the service between the preacher and the congregation.'*

Festivals

4.25   Festivals are an important part of the annual cycle of worship for deaf people. Those who normally worship in small congregations once a month in their own towns are able to come together to form a much larger group where there can be a different spirit in the worship. It is possible to invite visiting preachers which may not be appropriate with small congregations. In many dioceses festival services are held at Easter, Harvest and Christmas.

4.26   Where the regular services take place once a month, the pattern of the Christian year is difficult to maintain. For example when, as in 1996, Palm Sunday is the fifth Sunday of the month and there is no regular service on that day, should palms be blessed and distributed in one church on the second Sunday in Lent or Easter Sunday, together with the distributions at other churches on the third Sunday in Lent, Mothering Sunday and the fifth Sunday in Lent?

The occasional offices

4.27   For those deaf people who are within the Christian community the chaplain will normally baptise the children and adults as appropriate, prepare people for confirmation, lead the wedding services and take the funerals. This is the same as for any hearing community except that the normal place of worship for the deaf congregation may not be licensed for weddings.

4.28   However, if deaf people approach their parish clergy there may well be problems in communication. Most clergy are not competent to take a service for deaf people without advice. Parish clergy need to be in touch with the diocesan chaplain to discuss if it would be more appropriate for a person with signing skills to prepare people for the service and lead it, or if interpreters should be employed both at the meetings before the service and at the service itself. In this case there will be additional costs and the diocese should have a policy as to who should pay. It would be unfair for a church to charge more for the baptism, marriage or funeral of a deaf person than of a hearing person.

4.29   In some parishes before a baby is baptised the parents are asked to go for several weeks to services which are not interpreted. Many deaf people object to being asked to sit and watch others do something which is totally incomprehensible.

4.30   In the past, at funerals when close relatives of the deceased were deaf, they were left out of the preparations for the funeral and were unable to understand the funeral service unless it was taken by the chaplain among deaf people. There must be few clergy who when visiting the relatives of the bereaved ask if any of the relatives or friends are deaf. Yet if they do not ask they are unlikely to find out, and the deaf people will not receive the comfort or care that the Church should provide.

4.31   **We recommend that dioceses prepare a clear policy for the occasional offices for deaf people and publicise this policy to all the parish clergy.** (Recommendation 7)

Prayer groups and bible study

> '*I started a prayer group for deaf people. They found it strange as they had never prayed together before so they did not know where to look. Then I brought a candle for them to look at; I think it helped.*'

4.32   Some people used to think that deaf people could not participate in prayer groups or bible study. No reason was given but possibly it was because they had never done so in the past and nothing new was attempted in their churches. This is now changing, as small groups are starting to meet on weekday evenings to study the Scriptures and to pray, just as is happening in a growing number of churches for hearing people. Deaf people have to travel further but they are sufficiently keen to do so and will become the source of a new strength in the Church.

4.33   At present no part of the Bible is available in BSL, but the Bible Society is working to translate parts of the Scriptures on to a video and it will make a great practical difference when at least one gospel becomes available. It will be a symbol of the acceptance of deaf people within the family of the Church. It will be right that deaf people will be able to see the Scriptures in their own language.

4.34   Deaf people make use of their skills in story-telling to make the bible stories known to their own and the following generations. When the Bible is read in church or in a bible study, sign language makes the story come alive in a unique way.

CHAPTER 5

Ministry: Chaplains

> 'Deaf people need each other and need a pride in being who they are as the good creation of a loving God. We need to "hear the Word" in our own mother languages and to be encouraged to interpret the meaning of the Word within our own context. This means that deaf people are to pass from being objects of ministry to sharing in ministry, including the doing of theology and the shaping of the communities.'

5.1   In the Church of England the work of a minister among deaf people is fundamentally the same as that of a parish minister, but for specific people living across a wide area rather than for everybody in the immediate locality. The minister is responsible to the bishop for providing a wide range of pastoral care, both in the development and nurture of the worshipping communities of deaf people, and in pastoral care and evangelism to the wider, uncommitted communities of deaf people.

5.2   Traditionally the Church of England has offered a ministry to deaf people, trying to provide for their needs, and giving them the opportunity to receive the ministration of the Church. This top-down approach is no longer adequate. Deaf people see themselves, and are recognised to be, full members of the community. They expect to take full command of their own lives and to be offered and to accept appropriate leadership opportunities.

5.3   Chaplains should seek to encourage these attitudes of independence and self-determination among deaf Christians. They should seek to enable them to become full members of the Church and to obtain equality of opportunity, as well as developing leadership and ministerial

training. An increasing number of deaf people are responding to the call
to the different ministries in the Church.

5.4   The preferred terms today are 'chaplain among deaf people' and
'minister among deaf people' reflecting the description of a parish priest
as a minister 'among you as one who serves'.

5.5   Chaplains should try to develop ministerial teams to serve the
deaf community more effectively. Teams normally involve deaf people in
the roles to which they are called and for which they are trained. These
may include ordained, licensed or unofficial lay ministry.

5.6   The chaplain's prime tasks are as follows:

- to offer and maintain worship opportunities in sign language for
the deaf communities of the diocese;

- to develop the theological understanding of the congregations;

- to encourage and extend the spiritual life of deaf members of the
Church;

- to call forth and foster vocations from the community to the ministries of the Church;

- to promote the Gospel among the deaf communities of the
diocese;

- to provide opportunities for religious education for deaf children
and adults;

- to offer personal pastoral care in times of need;

- to offer the Occasional Offices;

- to form links between the deaf congregations and the diocese, and
to establish deaf people on electoral rolls, and within the synodical
structures of the diocese;

- to raise awareness at all levels of the diocese to the needs of deaf
people, to the contribution they can make to the life of the
Church and to enable true interaction to take place between deaf
and hearing people;

- to make expertise available to the parishes in all aspects of hearing impairment.

5.7   The way in which the chaplain works will vary according to local circumstances and the availability of ministers, ordained and lay, full-time and part-time, paid or voluntary. Geography, the spread of population and the location of deaf clubs all make a vast difference to the needs for ministry and the way it is provided. In practice the shape and scope of the ministry provided by a diocese are dependent on factors such as tradition, resources and the commitment of key people.

5.8   The chaplain has the responsibility of enabling the members of the deaf community to become full members of the Church and to take their full part in its activities of proclamation, fellowship and service. In order to achieve this, the first requirement is one of involvement in the lives of the people and an understanding of their situation. It also means that the chaplain needs to have a good working knowledge of sign language.

5.9   Where there is a dedicated chapel for deaf people, it can be the central focus for the life of prayer and worship in the community and stand as a witness to the presence of the Church in its midst. As the natural centre for services it will allow the celebration of weddings and the taking of funerals to happen within the community setting.

5.10   Where there is no chapel, services may be held in a secular area of the deaf club building and this works well in some places. In other places services are held in the local parish church. This can provide opportunities for building good relationships with the parish clergy and people and representatives of the hearing congregation can become involved in the worshipping life of the deaf community.

5.11   Whatever arrangements are made for worship, it is very important that the deaf Church community, the chaplain and all other ministers are recognised as a valid and vital part of the diocesan community.

Full-time chaplains

5.12   The traditional image of chaplains in the past was of the full-time chaplain/missioner working from a Mission for the Deaf and Dumb, employed by a Voluntary Society and often only very loosely connected to the diocese. It is doubtful if this system ever worked effectively across the country as a whole. (The term 'dumb' is no longer considered acceptable and has been replaced by 'without speech'.) Most chaplains are now employed by the diocese to give spiritual and pastoral care to deaf people and to lead their worship.

5.13   The advantages of chaplains being full-time include their clear commitment to the deaf community, the opportunity to develop skills in communication and their understanding of deaf culture. These three elements are essential to the work of any chaplain for the deaf and experience has shown that, for newly appointed chaplains coming from outside the deaf community, difficulties can arise if their loyalties are divided.

5.14   A main disadvantage of employing one chaplain full-time with responsibility for a whole diocese is the distance that needs to be travelled; chaplains may have to travel more than fifty miles in a day to lead worship, visit the sick or prepare people for baptism or confirmation. This is where the image of the chaplain being the 'vicar' for deaf people breaks down.

5.15   Another disadvantage of having just one chaplain is the danger of loneliness and isolation, particularly because a hearing chaplain is not always fully 'at home' in a deaf world. This sense of isolation is not inevitable and the need to mix with hearing colleagues can be met by attendance at the local deanery chapter, by co-operation with diocesan staff and by participation in diocesan events. The danger of isolation may be greater when the chaplain is employed by an independent organisation.

Part-time chaplains

5.16   There are few dioceses which are small enough for one part-time chaplain to provide an adequate level of ministry to the deaf community across the whole of the diocese. Where there are only one or two strong deaf clubs, which most of the deaf community attend, then it may be possible, but more often the part-time chaplain will require the support of a team of lay and ordained ministers. It is the responsibility of both the chaplain and the diocese to develop this team.

5.17   In the past, some part-time chaplains have been greatly disadvantaged from the start of their ministry because insufficient thought was given as to how they should start in their new post. A priest who has no knowledge of sign language will find it almost impossible to start learning to sign and at the same time to take on responsibility for a parish and the chaplaincy.

5.18   There is concern in the deaf community about the standard of signing by part-time chaplains. To reach a satisfactory standard requires either nine months' full-time study or three years' part-time study combined with frequent use of the language between classes. It is unfair to both the deaf community and the chaplain to expect ministry where there is no common means of communication.

Non-Stipendiary Ministers (NSMs)

5.19   Chaplains who are NSMs (like all NSMs) do not form a coherent group. Some who are employed as interpreters or as specialist workers with deaf people (e.g. by local Social Service or Education Departments) can bring skills which will enable them to work very effectively as chaplains, despite the constraints on the time they can give to the work.

5.20   Dioceses who are able to use the skills of such people will always have to ensure that the time the chaplain can give is adequate for the needs of the deaf community.

Honorary chaplains

5.21   This term is applied to some parish priests who give a small amount of their time and ministry to the deaf community within their ministry as a whole, and to priests who have retired but maintain this as one of their interests. They can form a valuable part of a ministry team, but cannot provide an adequate level of ministry on their own across a diocese.

Team ministry

5.22   There are several dioceses which are developing chaplaincy teams involving deaf and hearing people. This has the advantage of enabling the chaplains to live much closer to the people with whom they minister. A team can provide ministry even during a vacancy or holidays. A team enables the different skills of ordained and lay people to be fully used in the Church. Often Christians with great skills in working in a signing community are employed in Education and Social Services, and they can make a great contribution to the Church, each according to their gifts, if suitable training and support are provided.

5.23   It is important that all members of the team are trained to communicate and that they understand the culture of deaf people.

Chaplains who are deaf

5.24   There are at present three chaplains who are themselves deaf and three deaf students at theological college. The Committee for Ministry among Deaf People welcomes this development particularly because it provides a role model for other potential ministers and so encourages full participation by more deaf people. Inevitably some deaf people find it easier to talk to and confide in another deaf person. Deaf chaplains will provide a knowledge and understanding of deaf issues both for those who train with them and in meetings of chapters and synods.

Lay chaplains

5.25   There is a strong tradition of lay chaplaincy providing a very valuable part of the whole ministry of the Church. When a lay person is chaplain, it is important to ensure that there are priests available with adequate signing skills to administer the sacraments so that deaf people do not always receive the words of the sacrament second-hand through an interpreter.

5.26   As with all other lay ministries in the Church, it is important for the lay chaplain to be recognised by the diocese and accepted by the Church.

Chaplains in training

5.27   Very few dioceses have a post for a second chaplain specifically as a training post.

We recommend that all dioceses look to the future and consider what action is needed to ensure that trained chaplains will be available when vacancies occur. (Recommendation 3)

Chaplains in Training Programme

5.28   The Committee for Ministry among Deaf People (CMDP) has devised the Chaplains in Training Programme (CITP) to equip priests and other ministers to work effectively among deaf people.

5.29   The objective is to provide a course of training that allows the students, while working in the deaf community, to gain the knowledge of deafness and deaf people needed to minister effectively and using the situations and people they encounter to provide the basis of theological reflection.

5.30   The course involves in-service modular training supported by a tutorial system, the tutors being experienced chaplains, and an annual residential course, plus occasional study days on specific topics. The programme is candidate-led, in the sense that each person has a different working situation, and is able to devote different levels of commitment to the course.

5.31   CITP covers a variety of subjects including the nature of deafness, the variety of deaf people, the pastoral care of deaf people, communication skills needed for liturgy and pastoral care, ministerial practice in pastoral care of deaf people, and the education, sociology and psychology of deafness. In all modules the emphasis is on the impact these areas have on the acquisition and practice of faith.

5.32   Sign language and other communication skills are taught by other appropriate bodies using the Council for the Advancement of Communication with Deaf People's (CACDP) programme of assessment and qualification. It is expected that under normal circumstances a chaplain shall pass Stage Two of the CACDP qualifications (or equivalent) as a minimum standard necessary to work among deaf people. CITP does include the application of sign language to pastoral care and liturgy. CMDP is working with CACDP to produce a specialised module in this area.

5.33   CITP is divided into three stages: Introductory, Intermediate and Diploma. Negotiations are going on for the Diploma to be a university-accredited diploma. CMDP recommend that candidates should achieve the Introductory certificate within two years of appointment. Full-time chaplains should attain the Intermediate certificate within four years of appointment, while part-time and other chaplains will determine their pace according to their own circumstances.

5.34   CITP is organised and monitored by the Secretary to CMDP who is responsible to the CMDP Training sub-committee. In 1996, the cost was £300 per annum per candidate, which includes administration, tutors' expenses and attendance at the study days and the residential course.

5.35   In April 1996 there were 16 candidates studying for the Introductory Certificate, 18 for the Intermediate Certificate and 4 for the

Diploma. Since 1989 20 Introductory certificates, 10 Intermediate certificates and 9 Diplomas have been awarded.

5.36   **We recommend that the training of chaplains continue to be the responsibility of CMDP with the candidates supported and financed by their dioceses.** (Recommendation 11)

5.37   **We recommend that dioceses make it a condition of employment that stipendiary chaplains obtain Stage Two of the CACDP examination, or equivalent, and the CMDP chaplain's diploma within a fixed time of taking up their employment.** (Recommendation 8)

CHAPTER 6

Deaf lay ministry

> 'Deaf people preach with full facial expression, then the service is lively. The hearing person comes and preaches with a dead face — then it's boring.'

Ministry of deaf people

6.1   Deaf people are members of the whole Body of Christ, and as such are themselves called to minister within the Body.

6.2   The ministry of deaf people is usually exercised within the deaf worshipping communities, but this should not preclude deaf people from ministering within a congregation of hearing people. Such ministry can have a great influence on many people.

6.3   At present in the Church of England there are two priests and one deacon who are deaf and about 40 Readers. Many other deaf people exercise informal ministries within their own communities.

Selection and training

6.4   Those called to train for the ordained ministry are selected and trained through the normal diocesan and national systems of selection and training. Sign language interpreters are used when appropriate.

6.5   Those wishing to train for an accredited lay ministry, including that of a Reader, must also pass through normal diocesan systems. The Committee for Ministry among Deaf People (CMDP) offers a training course which is suitable both as a part of Reader training, and as training for other ministries, to equip those who seek to exercise lay ministry in the Church.

6.6   Since the language of many deaf people is British Sign Language, some candidates may have limited written English skills. Evaluation during selection and training, and the methods of training used should take this into account and make special provision for deaf candidates and students.

6.7   **We recommend that dioceses provide encouragement and financial resources for deaf people to be selected and trained for lay and ordained ministry.** (Recommendation 4)

6.8   The ministry of deaf people within the deaf community is vitally important for the following reasons:

●   They can provide the worshipping community with an appropriate role model, thus increasing the confidence of the community.

●   It is likely that a deaf minister will be able to communicate more effectively in sign language than a hearing minister, for whom sign language is a foreign language.

●   Pastoral care, evangelism and Christian nurture within the deaf community are all carried out more effectively by people for whom the community is 'home'.

●   The increase in the number of deaf people in ministry means that the Church among Deaf People has moved away from the 'Mission to the Deaf' perspective of previous years. Instead, a theologically aware and literate part of the Church is prepared to take responsibility for its own life and mission.

The Deaf Lay Ministry Training Programme

6.9   The Deaf Lay Ministry Training Programme (DLMTP) was developed by CMDP to meet the needs of deaf people responding to a call to ministry, and in particular to provide centralised training for them to fulfil their callings. It is not open to people with hearing.

6.10   Deaf people have been encouraged to accept liturgical tasks in their churches since the 1960s and there was a short training course for them at that time called the 'Deaf Lay Helpers Course'. By 1989 this was no longer appropriate and had ceased to operate. The then Ministry sub-committee of the General Synod Council for the Deaf, and later of CMDP, undertook a review of the situation and developed the present programme of learning for deaf people seeking a ministerial role.

6.11   The aim of the DLMTP is to develop a confident deaf Christian community able to express and defend the faith.

6.12   The objective is to help to equip deaf Christians for ministry among their own communities as Readers or Pastoral Assistants or in other roles, pastoral, teaching and liturgical. The number of candidates is small and because they are scattered across the whole country, no diocese has enough potential students or enough expert tutors to run a local course. The inter-relationship between students is an important part of the dynamics of training and this necessitates a group of at least 20, which can only be achieved on a national scale.

6.13   The content of the programme has been developed under the headings 'Being, Knowing and Doing', extending the candidates' self-knowledge as well as helping them to acquire the skills to minister.

6.14   The DLMTP makes its major input over three weekend courses each year, but is based on a partnership in learning between the candidate, the local chaplain and the programme leaders. The programme is intended to complement any training which is available locally. The chaplain is responsible for agreeing an appropriate personal pattern of prayer and bible reading with the candidate.

6.15   All candidates have to be approved and supported by their local chaplain and their local congregation. They are asked to draw up a 'ministerial contract' with the chaplain, and the appropriate diocesan officer, in order to establish what ministerial tasks they will undertake, and what training they need for these tasks. Each contract should be registered with the Secretary to CMDP and reviewed annually.

6.16   Candidates work between weekends under the guidance of their chaplains; they keep a written record/diary of their work and experience, and bring work to the weekends for review and assessment. This assessment is continuous and is part of the partnership between the candidate, the chaplain and local community and CMDP. Chaplains as part of their training are required to attend one DLMTP weekend in order to be properly equipped to support future candidates.

6.17 Candidates are expected to complete at least six out of the nine weekends in three years, chosen according to their training and development needs. People who want to train as Readers are expected to participate in all nine weekends, but this may be over a period longer than three years; they are also expected to take part in appropriate Reader training in their dioceses.

6.18 The training takes place within a structure of worship, study and leisure time, giving time for informal discussion and the exchange of ideas. All teaching is in sign language, given either directly by the tutor, usually a qualified and experienced chaplain, or through qualified sign language interpreters.

6.19 More than 40 people have taken part in the programme and 25 have been awarded certificates of completion. Follow-up courses are arranged from time to time, including a summer school in alternate years.

6.20 **We recommend that CMDP continue to be responsible for the management of the DLMTP with the candidates supported and financed by their dioceses.** (Recommendation 11)

The National Deaf Church Conference

6.21 The National Deaf Church Conference (NDCC) was founded in 1967 by the Revd Canon Tom Sutcliffe, who was himself deaf. It is the umbrella organisation of the Diocesan Deaf Church Conferences and is the platform for deaf Christians to have a voice within the Church in their own communities and the wider Church. Dioceses are each invited to send two representatives who, like the officers, are all themselves deaf.

6.22 The aims of the NDCC are to promote the Gospel among deaf people and to improve public awareness of their needs in worship. It also works towards encouraging fellowship amongst deaf people in the dioceses and their chaplains.

6.23 The activities of the NDCC involve twice-yearly conferences where deaf Christians discuss the spiritual and social issues facing the Church of England. It organises Deaf Choir Festivals, National Pilgrimages and Regional Eucharists. At all these events interpreters from among the chaplains play an important part interpreting for hearing speakers and congregations. Under its umbrella, the Association of Deaf Readers and Pastoral Assistants works to encourage and help deaf lay ministers.

6.24 The NDCC is funded from donations and fund-raising at conferences. At present the funding is insufficient to pay even the committee members' travel expenses. This means that the north and far west find it difficult to find representatives who can be members. Also, extra care needs to be taken to avoid having two meetings in a month, which would make it impossible for some people to afford to attend both. There is a need to find funds for expansion of the work and especially to develop more regional meetings for deaf people.

6.25 **We recommend that General Synod recognise the National Deaf Church Conference as the national organisation representing deaf people in the Church of England and provide adequate funding to extend its work throughout the country.** (Recommendation 12)

CHAPTER 7

Children and young people

'I see a lot of young people. I go into their world and invite them into our church. It is better that young and old worship together, then all can learn, meditate together and not just play pool. I spend time learning about the young community, what young people find important and how to minister to them. I like being with them and helping them.'

Learning about the faith

7.1   Children are naturally curious and want to explore what life is all about. Most children have the tools of hearing and sight which communicate what is happening and what it means. For children who are deaf it is more difficult; the basic values of life have to break through the communication barrier. Ways other than through speech have to be found to nurture the important elements of life such as love, learning to be independent, and learning to care for others, the environment and oneself.

7.2   This process starts within the family where children learn about self-awareness, development and worth, and where they experience love and care. Children need family life, with love and understanding as they set out on their journey of life.

7.3   For hearing parents of a deaf child the time when their supposedly normal child is first pronounced deaf can be a time of bewilderment, helplessness, frustration, grief and maybe anger. They may experience other feelings such as guilt or anxiety as to whether it is their fault. Some parents find it difficult to accept the full significance of the handicap and hope for years that the effects of deafness will diminish and that the child will develop normally. As the parents gradually come to terms with their child's disability they realise that they will have to use different ways of communicating with the child. They urgently need the opportunity to share their problems with other parents of deaf children and to meet deaf adults to learn where their child may be going. But too often these opportunities are not available. They may be seen only by professionals who may give good advice but cannot give the informal support that other parents receive from their neighbours and grandparents and all their other social relationships. Ideally it is at this stage that the chaplain first meets the family.

7.4   A child deaf from birth has never heard normal speech and so communication skills can be poorly developed or severely delayed. Although most deaf children can be taught to listen using modern hearing aids, what they hear will be very imperfect, depending on the severity of their deafness. Those with moderate hearing losses should learn to use their residual hearing through amplification and learn to speak and lip-read. This is known as learning through the oral method. For those with more severe hearing losses success through the oral method is much more difficult to achieve and a total communication approach may be used (signs, finger-spelling and spoken language) or sign language.

7.5   Hearing people wishing to work with deaf children should be flexible and be familiar with both British Sign Language (BSL) and Sign Supported English (SSE). In fact, most deaf children will use a quite sophisticated combination of methods and will respond warmly to any hearing person who makes an effort to communicate with them by whatever means, although they will particularly welcome those who can adapt their communication skills to the needs of the moment.

7.6   Some 10 per cent of deaf children have deaf parents. Signing is the normal means of communication in these families. The provision for the teaching of BSL to hearing parents is very varied across the country, ranging from excellent to none. Nevertheless, the deaf child lacks the informal learning which a hearing child receives from the sounds of voices surrounding them, a parent talking when cooking or washing the child, or when playing ball. It is hard to sign and catch a ball at the same time.

7.7   There are few things more frustrating than not understanding and not being understood. As deaf children grow up they need to relate and communicate with a wide variety of people, including young and old, to develop social skills. This cannot happen if they find themselves in a hearing community which cannot communicate with them. If they are to learn about life and death, good and bad, kindness and cruelty, they must be within their own culture, learning not only by being told but also by mixing with other deaf people, sharing their experience and seeing how they live.

7.8   Deaf children do not hear the word 'God' but they do acquire an understanding of the concept of God. How they learn to view God will depend on the attitudes and values which they personally adopt as having meaning and significance in their lives. The school through its morning assembly should offer a broad understanding of the meaning of worship and prayer, and the Religious Education curriculum will provide a wide perspective of the main religions of the world, with special emphasis on Christianity, and of the part the different religions have played and continue to play in the lives of individuals, groups and nations. Concrete facts are, for the most part, easily absorbed but an appreciation of the abstract and the spiritual is much more difficult due to the limitations in language development.

7.9   Deaf children attending residential schools spend over two-thirds of their time at the school and few have anything at all to do with the church. Many deaf children first attend a residential school as early as age 3 or 4 and stay until they are 16 when they go on to Further Education College for a few years. If the family have poor communication skills it is wishful thinking to expect them to play the key role in offering deaf children the very special environment where abstract and spiritual understanding can be experienced, developed and nurtured. There is a great challenge for deaf Christians and chaplains to work together to provide help, guidance, encouragement and support.

Schools

7.10   The methods used in the provision of education for deaf children vary across the country. There is still considerable controversy among educationalists in England regarding the best method of educating deaf children. Some schools use the oral method, whilst others use manual methods within a Total Communication environment. Some schools are now using a bilingual approach to Education, that is, BSL and English are taught as distinct languages. About 10 per cent of the children are in special schools for deaf children, the rest are in mainstream schools either in Partial Hearing Units or in the normal classes but with additional communication support.

7.11   To communicate with deaf children requires very special skills. The teacher needs to have very clear lip patterns when speaking and also to have good knowledge of sign language as well as an ability to understand the different modes and when to use them appropriately. To understand deaf children needs considerable experience and also a knowledge of each particular child. Deaf children learn to communicate at very different rates and on meeting them for the first time an adult needs to tune to the style of communication of each child.

7.12   The provision of chaplains, ordained or lay, at special schools for deaf children is probably at a very similar level to that in boarding schools for hearing children. Some schools have a very good chaplaincy arrangement with regular services and the children know the chaplains personally. The chaplain may be either one of the members of staff or the diocesan chaplain among deaf people or, in schools using the oral method, the local parish priest. Some schools have baptism preparation classes, confirmation classes, choirs and good pastoral care. Other schools, especially those which were not Christian foundations, have no chaplain. Even where there is good provision within the schools, the home dioceses need to make sure that they can follow up this work when the children are at home.

7.13   Normally, deaf children at mainstream day schools have the same provision for religious education as hearing children. With deaf children at possibly ten or more different schools in a diocese it is impossible for the chaplain to reach children through these schools.

The parish Church

> *'The young may not be interested now, but in time of trouble later they may want to come.'*

7.14   Very few parishes have a person skilled at working with deaf children as a member of the congregation. This makes the development of a national parish-based ministry to deaf children impossible. Parents are often unaware that the Church is concerned about the welfare of their deaf children. When parish priests know of deaf children they should seek the advice of the chaplain as to where there are resources available to help the families in the spiritual care of the children.

The diocese

> *'In London there may be many deaf young people; in the rural areas there are only a few.'*
>
> *'Could we have a one-day youth conference for young people?'*

7.15   In a recent survey seven dioceses were found which make specific provision for deaf children. Three Sunday Schools, one Monday School, a mother and toddler group, an annual Children's Day at a Deaf Centre with support from the Diocesan Children's Officer and a diocese which has special support for deaf children at some of the diocesan activities for children. In addition, some other dioceses do seek to include children at services for Mothering Sunday and Christmas.

7.16   There are major problems in developing a diocesan programme for deaf children: it is no longer easy for clergy to discover deaf children in their parish because of the confidentiality imposed on social workers and others; there is a great lack of skilled adults or teachers, and the children may have to travel a considerable distance if a viable group is to be formed. It is most unlikely that a satisfactory programme of regular weekly or monthly Sunday activities for deaf children is ever going to be developed in every diocese, but there is much scope for making more of the activities provided for hearing children accessible for deaf children.

7.17   However, at diocesan youth events it is possible to develop communication support for deaf young people. During the past few years Colleges of Higher Education and universities have greatly increased this support for deaf young people. There is no reason why the Church should not start to follow this example. If dioceses have too few deaf young people to develop a viable programme then work needs to be started on developing a regional programme. It is doubtful if many Diocesan Youth Officers have attended deaf awareness courses, but their expertise is needed together with the skills of the chaplaincy team to enable young people to grow in the faith.

7.18   **We recommend that dioceses review their provision for the spiritual care for deaf children and young people.** (Recommendation 9)

National Anglican organisations

> Q. *'How can we integrate young people into the Church?'*
>
> A. *'Could we have a week at Glastonbury for young people?'*

7.19   We are not aware of any of the national Anglican organisations having a special concern for deaf children or young people. Those Christian organisations which run summer camps and similar activities make no provision for the special communication needs of deaf people, although some have done so in the past. This is regrettable. There are enough enquiries from parents about activities for their children for a viable number to be invited to the national activities.

7.20 **We recommend that national Anglican organisations which run activities for children and young people provide skilled communicators in order to allow deaf children and young people to participate.** (Recommendation 10)

CHAPTER 8

Hard of hearing, deafened and deafblind people

The Minister shall read with a loud voice ...

The Minister shall kneel, and say ... with an audible voice ...

He that readeth, so standing and turning himself,

as he may best be heard of all such as are present.

(Morning Prayer. *The Book of Common Prayer*)

People who are hard of hearing

8.1   People who are hard of hearing have difficulty in understanding speech, but it is not impossible. Courtesy and consideration greatly reduce the difficulties. It is difficult for those who hear well to understand the frustration of the hard of hearing when most of the people around can understand what is being said and they are unable to do so. A burden, which could be eliminated if people took more care, can be heavier than one which is unavoidable.

8.2   As the Prayer Book makes clear, it is the responsibility of the minister to ensure that the service can be heard and understood by everyone present. It is a very unusual congregation in which every member has good hearing. Attendance without understanding is not the tradition of the Church of England.

8.3   The hard of hearing rely on their remaining hearing and sight to understand what is being said. So anyone leading worship should be clearly visible and well lit. There may well be good liturgical reasons for reading the Gospel or intercessions from the middle of the congregation,

45

but there are better liturgical reasons for ensuring that the reader can be heard by all the congregation.

8.4   Churches which are not small need a sound enhancement system. But all churches need a loop system to enable those who rely on their hearing aid to hear all that is said. Loudspeakers and loops are useless without adequate microphones. Either the minister needs a radio microphone or there should be standing microphones at least in the pulpit, at the lectern, Communion Table, vicar's stall, front step of the chancel, font, crib, Easter garden, west door (if there is an Easter Procession), vestry door (if the first hymn is announced from there), and any other place from which people speak to the congregation.

8.5   When anything is being read or said in church, if it is worth saying, it should be spoken clearly. If it is not clear, then it is better not said. At all services, but in particular family and children's services, care needs to be taken as to who is asked to read the lessons or lead the prayers. Some young people have beautiful clear voices, well trained, which are a pleasure to listen to.

8.6   There is no reason why the hard of hearing should not be enabled to participate fully in the worship in the same way as hearing people. It needs thought, care and preferably an element of love.

8.7   In those church halls which have no loop system the leaders at a meeting need to remember that the understanding of speech is made much harder if there is background noise. This may come from a kitchen, an adjoining hall or elsewhere and should be eliminated if possible. But a greater trouble can come at meetings which split up into small groups, while remaining in one room. Even those with only a small hearing loss can find it impossible to follow a discussion in such situations.

8.8   We include in Appendix B on p.73 advice on talking to people who are deafened, and the same advice applies when talking to those who are hard of hearing.

Deafened people

8.9   Deafened people suffer from isolation. Before losing their hearing they used to move easily in society and now are cut off from their previous main means of communication. If the loss of hearing is sudden, it always takes a considerable time to start to make the necessary adjustments to their way of living. This is not made easier by those who act as if a person who cannot hear, cannot think.

8.10   Because there are only a very few deafened people there is no community of people who have the same challenges. There are no local clubs, no local societies, no churches where all the other members are deafened.

8.11   Some partially deafened people can develop their lip-reading skills so that they can take part in a one-to-one conversation in good conditions. But group meetings are impossible, without a notetaker or voice to text interpreting. For many deafened people ten minutes of a speech leaves them tense and frustrated. Under these conditions the brain works less well. It is unfortunate that the harder one tries to lip-read, the less one can comprehend. People who are tense find lip-reading becomes much harder. This is a problem at bereavement visits and when discussing family problems.

8.12   To be deafened is like being a goldfish in a bowl. You can see what is happening all around but you cannot take part in it. Sometimes a helper will write something, and show it to you, which helps you to understand, but this can make you feel even more of an outsider.

8.13   Provided the preacher and those leading the intercessions and other variable parts of the service prepare by writing out what they will say, it is relatively easy to give a copy of the full written service to a deafened person. But to have to read while all around are listening is a cold, unemotional experience. It is better for an experienced notetaker to sit beside the deafened person so as to give them an outline of the sermon and prayers. But a bad notetaker is of no more use that an inaudible reader.

8.14   For a service where a large number of deafened people are present, a voice to text interpretation projected onto a large screen is always the most useful way of allowing all to participate in the service. But this is relatively expensive. An overhead projector, with an efficient operator, can be used to good effect at a much lower cost, but it requires good preparation.

8.15   At first in a personal ministry it may not be easy to become accepted without appearing patronising. It takes time to break down the non-communication barrier. The most important thing is to maintain eye contact and this can be difficult if there is no response. Care with all the items listed in Appendix B together with paper and pen at hand and a relaxed manner are essential.

8.16   Deafened people soon learn that social gatherings emphasise their isolation. Churches need to be sensitive in helping those who have lost their hearing to the same extent as they are sensitive to those who are bereaved.

8.17   Within the family there is the danger that because their partner is with them for much of the time, private forms of communication develop and so it is easy to become dependent on the partner for all communication needs. A stranger talks to the partner who relays the information. It is easier that way, but totally destructive of personality.

Deafblind people

8.18   There are 16 dioceses which make specific provision for the worship and pastoral care of people who are deafblind.

8.19   Deafblind people know only what they are told by touch, what they smell, taste or feel. They are normal human beings who need a little bit of extra help. Deafblindness is a disability which cuts off most communication with the immediate environment and with the wider world beyond.

8.20   Deafblind people may have been born deafblind, been born deaf and lost their sight, been born blind and lost their hearing, or born seeing and hearing and then lost these faculties in turn. Every deafblind person is an individual and they all have their own experiences on which they can draw to understand the world around them.

8.21   Deafblind people may receive information from other people by means of the deafblind manual alphabet, Block, visual frame signing, hands-on signing, Braille, Moon or Tadoma (for definitions see Glossary). They may communicate by speech, deafblind manual alphabet, Block, British Sign Language, Makaton or any combination of these. They may write using a Braille or Moon typewriter and communicate at a distance using a text-telephone with Braille pad receiver.

8.22   In effect, all communication with deafblind people is one-to-one. At a service or a meeting each person will have an interpreter or communicator.

8.23 Meeting deafblind people takes time and sensitivity. What deafblind people most lack is information. They have no newspapers, television or radio to describe what is happening in the world. They lack the normal awareness of their surroundings, unless they are in a familiar environment. For many there is the danger of loneliness, isolation, withdrawal, frustration. There are the problems of retaining independence and competence in daily living, obtaining access to activities and events. There is a need for deafblind people to meet with other people with the same disability to build friendships and to socialise with each other. A life limited to contact with carers is grossly deficient.

8.24   Those who were born deafblind may lack understanding about the people they meet. They may lack an understanding of birth, growing up, love, marriage and death having learnt of the world about them only by means of touch. On the other hand, other deafblind people have a better understanding of many things in the physical world, and the spiritual world, than those who see and hear. They may have used their time to think, rather than rushing to acquire a knowledge of the material things.

8.25   Ministry to deafblind people requires care and training. Many images of God may be inappropriate: 'Christ the light of the world', 'I heard the voice of the Lord'. Few of our images of God involve touch. It requires skill and imagination to explain the full meaning of Christmas, Lent, Good Friday, Easter, the resurrection, the ascension, the Trinity, or salvation in words whose meaning can be explained only using touch.

8.26   In the structure of the Church, ministry to deafblind people is normally considered to be the responsibility of the chaplain to the deaf community. When the deafblind person is integrated in the deaf community, this is clearly right. But many deafblind people have no connection with this community. It is totally unrealistic to expect a chaplain who has responsibility for people who live over a very wide area to be able to exercise a personal one-to-one pastoral ministry to all the deafblind people in the diocese. This responsibility must be accepted by people who live near, with advice being given by the chaplain.

CHAPTER 9

The responsibility of the dioceses

> Q. *'What do you expect of the hearing church?'*
>
> A. *'I expect them to know that deaf people exist. I often feel that the deaf Church is on its own. I would like to link with a hearing Church. Perhaps the hearing Church is not interested in the deaf Church. I think the bishops should take more interest in the deaf Church.'*

Identifying the challenge

9.1   There is a challenge to the Church at the present time to reconsider its responsibility to its deaf members. On the one hand, some deaf members of the Church feel neglected, undervalued, isolated and misunderstood and, on the other hand, some hearing members of the Church feel bewildered, helpless and possibly guilty at their failure to accept all members of the Church as equals. For hearing people the challenge of deafness can be rather remote, for deaf people it is always present.

Understanding the gifts and the needs of deaf people

9.2   It is always difficult to compare the gifts of two groups of people. Many of those who work with both deaf and hearing people consider that the eyesight of many deaf people is better trained than for hearing people. Deaf people see pictures more clearly and so have a special skill at storytelling. They see people more clearly and so are often more aware as to how a person is feeling. Their gifts of imagination can make worship more colourful, and more interesting with more movement and life.

9.3   Sign language can be read by anyone in a room so deaf people are more open in their conversations. Touch is an accepted means of communication among deaf people and many hearing people could learn from them how to reach out to those who feel lonely, isolated, unloved or unwanted by the world today.

9.4   Most members of the Church have no experience of meeting deaf or deafblind people. Many Parochial Church Councils (PCC) take seriously their responsibility to cater for people with physical disabilities so that they can join in parish worship, especially by providing wheelchair ramps and special toilets. In recent years many churches have been fitted with loop systems to enable people with hearing aids to take part in worship, but often those responsible are unable to be certain that they are effective and that they are used properly by the ministers. Sometimes it is true that the system is not switched on for every service.

9.5   Where loops have been fitted, the PCC may think that it has dealt with the problem of deafness, not realising that while they have helped the numerically largest group, those who are hard of hearing, they have not started to help the deaf, deafened and the deafblind.

9.6   The barrier between deaf and deafblind people and hearing people is the problem of communication. Normally for the Church if there is a problem of communication, it is with people who do not want to hear. The need is for speaking and writing in such a way that people will become interested. The Church should be experts at this. With deaf and deafblind people the problem is different, it is the mode of communication which needs to be altered. In conversation and in services the communication must be by sign language, notetaking or deafblind manual.

9.7   As long as the special gifts of deaf people are ignored or under-used, the Church is impoverished. On the other hand, the Church will lose its contact with deaf people if it fails to cater adequately for their needs, and they will take their needs, and their gifts, elsewhere. There is a growing number of people developing good signing skills among the Mormons and the Jehovah's Witnesses and they may become an attractive alternative to the Church of England.

9.8   We recommend that the Church of England at national and diocesan level takes responsibility for helping people to appreciate the gifts and to understand the needs of all deaf people, and for putting energy and resources, people and finance, into using these gifts and meeting these needs. (Recommendation 1)

Practical measures for integrating Church life and worship

'Some preachers do not like to give a written copy of their sermon to anyone before the service. So they may say, "The explorer slowly made his way forward". The interpreter uses the actions of a man hacking his way through the jungle. The preacher continues, "The snow on the ground became thicker and thicker." The interpreter changes to the actions of a man skiing. Many English words have different sign language equivalents according to the context. The interpreter needs to know the context before the service starts.'

9.9   Deaf people need ministers who can use sign language so that they can watch and understand the words and action of the liturgy. When someone has to act as an interpreter the deaf people need to watch the interpreter and so, because they cannot at the same time look at the minister, the actions at the altar, the movement in the sanctuary, even the use of visual aids is missed. Worship becomes second-hand.

9.10   When the idea of holding integrated services is first introduced, most hearing congregations will have to be helped to realise what provision is necessary for deaf people. Not only must a skilled interpreter be provided on a regular basis, and at least occasionally a priest who is proficient in sign language, but also deaf people should take their turn in leading parts of the service, at those points using the interpreter for the benefit of hearing members of the congregation. Interpreters need to be given details of the service several days in advance, including texts of the liturgy, readings, prayers and the sermon so that they can be well prepared; the abstract concepts of theological language have to be correctly translated into signs to give the full meaning in a way that is devotionally helpful. The speed of speech and sign are different. The minister and readers need to agree on a suitable compromise with the interpreter. Deaf people need to have a clear view of the minister and interpreter, in good light, not in front of a window or against a visually disturbing background nor with a high lectern obstructing their sight.

9.11   The life of a Church is not limited to worship on Sundays; most congregations nowadays have social and learning programmes, but not many ensure that this is available to everyone regardless of disabilities. Bible study, prayer groups, Mothers' Union, Mens' Fellowship and the annual pantomime, are all of interest to deaf people. In addition to these formal or semi-formal meetings, there is often an informal network of Christians visiting each other's homes. There is no reason why deaf, deafened or deafblind people should be excluded from this network, but it will not be accessible to them unless proper provision is made for adequate interpretation.

9.12   The basic pastoral needs of deaf people in times of birth, marriage, illness and bereavement are not very different from those of hearing people, but these needs are complicated by deafness itself, and by the lack of consideration often shown by other agencies. (See paragraphs 4.27–4.31 above.)

9.13   Dioceses have begun to hold race awareness seminars for clergy and lay people; deaf awareness sessions can be equally helpful in increasing understanding.

Wider provision of resources

> *'Funding is a problem which the hearing Church does not understand. Deaf people are so dispersed. They spend their money travelling to the services. There is no group of people living round the church who give money as with a parish church. Many deaf people are on low incomes. There is always the collection but monthly services with small congregations mean low collections.'*

9.14   Some diocesan officials understand and are working to cater for the needs of the deaf and hard of hearing communities. Some others still do not understand that many deaf people are 'unchurched' and have no access to worship or Christian pastoral care. If a hearing congregation loses its incumbent, there are alternative ministers working in the next parish. If there is no chaplain or if the post is reduced to part-time, ministers who can communicate in sign language are so few and far apart that the congregations of deaf people can be completely deprived of ministry and opportunities for appropriate corporate worship and pastoral care for a long time.

9.15   Since deaf people are only a small minority of the population, the congregation is inevitably very scattered; this poses its own problems for the chaplain in terms of travel and time commitment. Where a chaplain has responsibility for a whole diocese, a single bereavement visit can take a whole morning. If deaf people go into hospital or into prison, the (hearing) chaplain is not able to hold a proper conversation with them and the chaplain among deaf people is asked to visit. It is important that dioceses understand that a chaplain's 'parish' is very different from that of an incumbent, and make adequate provision.

9.16   **We recommend that every diocese should appoint an adequate number of ministers to enable the worship and pastoral care of the deaf community.** (Recommendation 2)

Diocesan structures

> 'Deaf people should be part of the structure of the Church. The deaf Church is marginalised and needs to be brought into the parish system.'

9.17   Chaplains benefit from being part of deanery chapters and/or ecumenical meetings and have their own contribution to make to these bodies, not least in helping the rest of the Church to understand the special circumstances of those who are deaf, deafened, hard of hearing and deafblind.

9.18   Deaf people have an equal right with hearing people to take a part in the councils and synods of the Church. What they have to contribute should be recognised, e.g. by including representatives of the deaf congregation in the appointment procedures for a new chaplain or minister.

9.19   **We recommend that dioceses enable deaf people to be full members of synods with appropriate provision of interpreters.** (Recommendation 5)

9.20   There are different ways of showing the love of Christ to people. One is by spending time with them, listening to them, sharing their joy and sadness. Another is by providing for their immediate needs – practical, emotional, material and spiritual. Another is by giving them political support, fighting with them for justice and against discrimination. Yet another is by receiving and valuing what they have to contribute to the whole community.

9.21   Most dioceses support the work of the chaplain among deaf people by means of an informal support group or a specific committee attached to the Board/Council for Ministry. The tasks of such a committee are to promote the interests of the deaf people in the diocese and to provide practical and financial resources to enable the chaplain to minister effectively. (See Appendix C on p.76).

9.22   It is vitally important for its own wholeness that the Church, both nationally and within each diocese, takes seriously the existence of deaf and deafblind people as members of the Body of Christ. It means becoming more aware of their special gifts and their special needs and doing everything possible both to maximise the gifts and to meet their needs.

9.23   **We recommend that dioceses ensure that chaplains among deaf people have adequate support in the form of a committee linked to one of the main synodical diocesan boards or councils and that specialised in-service training for the chaplains is encouraged and included in their committee budgets.** (Recommendation 6)

CHAPTER 10

Theological reflections

The problem comes not in deafness, but in fallen humanity's alienation from the intentions of our loving God. Such belief liberates deaf people to be ourselves trusting that our gifts have a vital role to play in the world. Indeed, the community of good creation is not complete without us. Nor is the community of God's children complete without the participation of any of the so-called minorities.

(Weir, 1996: p. 8)

'The problem comes not in deafness'

10.1   We believe in a God who communicates, God who became flesh and showed the visible sign of his practical, costly love for all people. All people includes deaf people. Not only is Jesus flesh and sign, he is also the Light, which the darkness never has, and never can, extinguish.

10.2   For everyday communication deaf people need the light. They must be able to see adequately to exchange information or pleasantries, express love and despair, and seek guidance or give help. God has arranged his creation so that deaf people can be fully part of it and play their part in the totality of what Weir calls 'the community of good creation'. She asserts that without deaf people the community is incomplete, the world and the Church are the less.

10.3   Isaiah foresaw that one of the marks of the new Kingdom would be that the deaf would hear. Jesus said to the disciples of John the Baptist: 'Go back and tell him what you are hearing and seeing, the blind can see, the lame can walk, ... *the deaf hear.*' A block to the completion of that Kingdom is the exclusion of deaf people from its community, by not

58

enabling them to see or 'hear' its message of Good News. 'The deaf *hearing*' is still a sign of the coming of the Kingdom, and that 'hearing' necessitates the provision of the opportunity to receive the Good News and share in its enactment in ways that are open to deaf people. In practice, a church without Ministry among Deaf People, or with a ministry offered by people not thoroughly competent in sign language, is maintaining 'fallen humanity's alienation from the intentions of our loving God'.

'The intentions of our loving God'

10.4   The story of the healing of the deaf man also helps us realise something of the nature of God. From it we learn that God understands the nature of deafness, and the needs of deaf people. Jesus was immediately aware of what he had to do to help the man brought before him. Jesus had to give him personal attention, and used a language mode that he could follow, and that enabled him to comprehend the presence before him, and the power to heal and save. All people need specific personal attention and, from this and the other healing miracles, we can see that Jesus was able to deal appropriately with each one individually and personally. He could touch the untouchable, include the outcast, recognise the possessed, and forgive the sinful. We learn that our God knows and meets our very personal needs and can deal with whatever concern or condition we might have.

10.5   Moreover, God created all people including those who are deaf. Psalm 139 makes it clear that neither light nor dark affect God. He is able to enter the world of those who are blind, so he must be able to enter the world of deaf people, because just as light and dark are alike to God, so sound and silence are alike to him.

'Such belief liberates deaf people to be ourselves'

10.6   The Church which accepts the call to present its Good News to deaf people will not be one that only gives. That would be to repeat the mistakes of the past. Instead, it will want to enable and empower deaf people themselves to give by playing a full part in the life and ministry of the Church. In this way deaf people will be able to:

- *proclaim* the Good News to others;

- *share* fully in the fellowship of the church community;

- *lead* its worship and develop liturgies that are suitable for sign language and full visual presentation;

- *serve* alongside their hearing peers as members of the servant community of the faith.

'Trusting that our gifts have a vital role to play in the world'

10.7   There are specific gifts that deaf people bring to the rest of the Church. Those who experience worship in the company of deaf people see afresh the drama and excitement of liturgy, as it unfolds before their eyes. To sit up and see, instead of bowing in personal private prayer, enhances the sense of community at worship. It brings to life the power of the saving acts of God shared by all present.

10.8   The graceful nature of sign language can provide beauty that matches the beauty of the sounds of music in worship, thus providing another dimension to refresh and stimulate the vision of God.

10.9   From more than one point of view deafness and deaf people bring a different perspective to life, especially to life in the faith community. Because of the way society and the Church tend to behave, deaf people are often pushed to the margin and made to feel excluded from many things. Yet this is the very place that Jesus chose to be in his life and ministry. This perspective, this point of view, is too easily lost in mainstream Church life today. Many deaf people come to faith and belief without much of the technical and literate circumstances of modern society. Their relationship with God, and his with them, is often untrammelled by detail or the complexities of knowledge or understanding. Often their faith is direct, clear and simple, but very powerful because it feels, to those who know them, like the faith Jesus calls for – the faith that is childlike in its openness and trust.

'Nor is the community of God's children complete . . .'

10.10   It is natural for deaf people to feel that they are a community. They should be free to meet and share that community life together. The Church may rejoice in this living example of the kind of community that the Church itself ought to be. However, the very community life of deaf people is under threat. This threat has come because of the *diaspora*, the scattering of deaf children through hearing schools and because many deaf adults are unaware of the opportunities of meeting other deaf people. Many other factors threaten this community life, but the Church should regard it as precious and help it to survive and grow. In essence, the coming together of deaf people is an act of pastoral care, a proclamation of the Kingdom afresh both among people who are deaf, and by example, among those who are not.

10.11   This part of the community of God's children is a very vibrant and dynamic one. It feels the strength and weakness of being a small minority, and is also bound together by a common purpose and identity, as a group sharing a common difficulty and a common sense of being 'outside'. One of its strengths is the sense of joint fellowship and loyalty. One of its beauties is its language and tradition of story-telling in a community and culture that are not dependent on a written tradition. In the deaf communities we can find the telling and sharing of stories such as the elders of the Church would have known. Signing brings a vividness and drama that make our readings of the Bible come alive.

'. . . without the participation of any of the so-called minorities'

10.12   A deaf person becomes a member of the community of deaf people by using sign language. In recent years this has been identified as a true language and is studied and researched in the same way as other languages and cultures. Hands are essential to all communication within this community in a totally different way from that within the oral cultures of the hearing world.

10.13 In a seminary in Katowice in Poland there is a crucifix, where Christ is held aloft, away from the Cross, with his wounded hands raised in a blessing. In the act of crucifixion, Christ's hands were brutalised and fixed to the Cross in a way designed to ensure they could never work again. In his case, work included blessing, feeding, healing, forgiving and raising the dead. His hands communicated the love of God to the deaf man and the many others he met on the way. Not even the worst that 'fallen humanity's alienation from the intentions of our loving God' could do could prevent for long those hands from their blessed work. They are liberated to bless, just as the Katowice Crucifix shows.

10.14 For many years the Church kept alive the use of sign language in its liturgy and worship when many were trying to deny it to deaf people. Now the Church can both liberate the hands of deaf people to proclaim his Kingdom to today's generation and welcome them into its fullest fellowship as members together of the one Body.

Chapter 11

Recommendations

We recommend that:

1. The Church of England at national and diocesan level takes responsibility for helping people to appreciate the gifts and to understand the needs of all deaf people, and for putting energy and resources, people and finance, into using these gifts and meeting these needs. (Paragraph 9.8)

2. Dioceses appoint an adequate number of ministers to enable the worship and pastoral care of the deaf community. (Paragraph 9.16)

3. Dioceses look to the future and consider what action is needed to ensure that trained chaplains will be available when vacancies occur. (Paragraph 5.27)

4. Dioceses provide encouragement and financial resources for deaf people to be selected and trained for lay and ordained ministry. (Paragraph 6.7)

5. Dioceses enable deaf people to be full members of synods with appropriate provision of interpreters. (Paragraph 9.19)

6. Dioceses ensure that chaplains among deaf people have adequate support in the form of a committee linked to one of the main synodical diocesan boards or councils and that specialised in-service training for the chaplains is encouraged and included in their committee budgets. (Paragraph 9.23)

7. Dioceses prepare a clear policy for the occasional offices for deaf people and publicise this policy to all the parish clergy. (Paragraph 4.31)

8.   Dioceses make it a condition of employment that stipendiary chaplains obtain Stage Two of the CACDP examination, or equivalent, and the CMDP chaplain's diploma within a fixed time of taking up their employment. (Paragraph 5.37)

9.   Dioceses review their provision for the spiritual care for deaf children and young people. (Paragraph 7.18)

10.   National Anglican organisations which run activities for children and young people provide skilled communicators in order to allow deaf children and young people to participate. (Paragraph 7.20)

11.   The Committee for Ministry among Deaf People continue to be responsible for the management of the training of chaplains and deaf lay ministers, with the candidates supported and financed by their dioceses. (Paragraphs 5.36 and 6.20)

12.   General Synod recognise the National Deaf Church Conference as the national organisation representing deaf people in the Church of England and provide adequate funding to extend its work throughout the country. (Paragraph 6.25)

Appendix A

Glossary

Association of Deaf Readers and Pastoral Assistants (ADRPA): A group within the National Deaf Church Conference which works to train and develop the ministry of its members.

Bilingual education: Bilingual education is an approach to the education of deaf children which respects and uses both the sign language of the deaf community and the spoken and written language of the hearing community.

Block: A method of communicating with a deafblind person by writing individual letters on the palm of their hand using a standard direction and sequence of strokes when forming the letters. The communicator uses one finger to write the letters. Normally used with people who could read before losing their sight.

Braille: A method of printing for blind people to read by touch. Letters are made of different combinations from six raised dots for each letter of the alphabet.

British Sign Language (BSL): British Sign Language is a language in its own right using manual signs, facial expression and body movement. BSL has its own grammatical structure and vocabulary. It is the natural language for most deaf people. It is not an easy language for hearing people to learn after childhood. It is not possible to use spoken language at the same time as signing BSL and so it is not suitable for a mixed group of signing people and non-signing hearing people or lip-readers.

CACDP: see **Council for the Advancement of Communication with Deaf People.**

Chaplain: A person, ordained or lay, who holds a licence from their bishop to minister among deaf people.

Chaplains in Training Programme: See paras 5.28–5.35.

Committee for Ministry among Deaf People: A sub-committee of the Advisory Board of Ministry to the General Synod of the Church of England which is responsible for the development of the Church among Deaf People and for the training of chaplains and deaf lay people.

Communication Support Worker: A BTEC qualification for those people who work as a member of a team assisting deaf people who are studying in Higher or Further Education.

Communicator: Normally an unqualified person who works to aid communication between deaf and hearing people.

Council for the Advancement of Communication with Deaf People (CACDP):

CACDP works to develop all forms of communication with deaf and deafblind people. It maintains a directory of registered interpreters and develops schemes of training and conducts examinations in:

 British Sign Language

 Communication and Guiding Skills with Deafblind People

 Deaf Awareness

 Interpreting

 Lip-speaking

 Speech to Text Reporting.

CACDP	**Stage 1**	Introductory examination.
	Stage 2	A pass in this intermediate examination indicates the ability to carry on a conversation.
	Stage 3	A pass in this advanced examination indicates fluency in the language.

Council on Deafness: An umbrella body of 33 organisations in the United Kingdom who work to assist deaf people.

Deaf: Deafness and the ability to understand speech cannot be measured on a simple scale. The ability to hear depends on the pitch and volume of the sound and the amount of background noise. For most people the ability to hear is different in each ear. The ability to understand speech also depends on how tired a person is, their state of health and many other factors. Every person is different.

There are many different ways of defining deafness and partial deafness. Deaf people are divided into different categories for different purposes – audiometry, medical, education, employment, etc. For each of these purposes the professionals dispute the different boundaries. However, in this book we use four expressions to describe groups of people with impaired hearing:

1. Deaf

2. Deafened

3. Hard of hearing

4. Deafblind

We use the word 'deaf' for people who, even if using a hearing aid, cannot understand speech by recognising the sounds and who lost this ability either at birth or before they could speak. Their preferred method of communication is often British Sign Language. This is a visual language used by deaf people in England.

Some people who are born deaf are not given the opportunity to learn sign language and so their communication with all other people may be restricted. There is no exact method of estimating the number of deaf people in any community but in England it is estimated that about 1 person in 1,000 of the total population is deaf.

Deafblind: We use the word 'deafblind' for people whose combined sight and hearing loss causes difficulty with communication, access to information and mobility. Using this broad definition there are about 40 people in every 100,000 of the population with dual sensory loss. Relatively few of these will have total loss of sight and hearing.

Deafblind manual: A means of communication, in which the communicator touches different parts of the receiver's hand to indicate the different letters of the alphabet. The fastest speed which can be achieved is about 50 words per minute, so at a public meeting an interpreter has to *précis* what is being said.

Deafened: The word 'deafened' is used for people who, even if using a hearing aid, cannot understand speech by recognising the sounds, and who lost this ability after they could speak. Some deafened people retain the ability to speak, others lose it. Some deafened people rely on lip-reading to understand speech.

On the other hand, some people who have lost their hearing, learn to use sign language, join the deaf community and are recognised as 'deaf'. Under the age of 65 the number of people who are deafened is about 1 person in 10,000. Over the age of 65 the number rapidly increases.

The Deaf Lay Ministry Training Programme: See paras 6.9–6.20.

Finger-spelling: A means of communication in which the communicator signs each letter of every word using standard positions of the fingers for each letter.

Hands-on signing: A means of communication in which the communicator uses the usual British Sign Language signs but the receiver places their hands over the communicator's hands to receive the signs. Hands-on signing is mainly used by deafblind people who learnt sign language before losing their sight.

Hard of hearing: We use the words 'hard of hearing' for people who, even if using their hearing aid, have difficulty in understanding speech.

About 17 per cent of the population are hard of hearing. The incidence increases with age, so that under the age of 60 about 1 person in 8 is hard of hearing and over that age 1 in 3. In an average congregation of 100, mostly elderly, at least 30 will have difficulty in understanding speech.

HiLink: A speech to text system where the operator uses a standard keyboard to produce a *précis* of speech. Normally used to give both a visible display and printed copy.

Interpreter: An interpreter passes messages from people using sign language to spoken English and vice versa. Interpreters use their skill and knowledge of the two different languages and cultures to receive a message given in a source language and pass it on in the target language. Registered Qualified and Trainee Interpreters are obliged to follow the CACDP Code of Practice.

Lip-reading: The skill of understanding speech by watching the movement of the lips but without hearing the sound. Very few people can understand more than 40 per cent of what is said by lip-reading alone. However, aided by residual hearing or by the use of other clues, body movement, facial expression and manual gestures, lip-reading helps many people to communicate.

Lip-speaker: A lip-speaker conveys a speaker's message to lip-readers accurately using unvoiced speech. Lip-speakers are normally used at meetings where lip-readers are likely to be too far from the speaker to be able to understand them directly.

Loop: A wire running round a room which creates an electric field so that speech through the microphone can be clearly heard through hearing aids which have been switched to receive from the loop. All churches and halls can be provided with loop systems and adequate microphones. When a hearing aid is switched to loop, the person using it will only receive sounds picked up by the microphones.

Makaton: A signing system comprised of a specially selected vocabulary of the most essential words. Makaton was devised to be used as an aid in the teaching of deaf people with learning disabilities. It is now also used with non-communicating hearing children and adults.

Moon: A method of printing for blind people to read by touch. Letters are made from different combinations of raised lines and semi-circles for each letter of the alphabet. To read Moon requires a less sensitive sense of touch than Braille.

National Deaf Church Conference (NDCC): The National Body composed of two deaf people from each diocese who represent the deaf community within the Church of England (see paragraphs 6.21–6.25). It has representation on the Committee for Ministry among Deaf People.

Notetaker: A person who assists a deaf person to understand speech by writing notes. This may be to produce a *précis* of what has been said or just to clarify individual words.

Oral method of education: A method of teaching deaf children using only lip-reading and no manual signs. Used universally from 1880 to about 1970 when it was found that the average reading skills of deaf children on leaving school was that of a 9-year-old child. Still used with children who have some residual hearing and in schools which continue a policy of oral education.

Paget Gormet: An aid to teaching deaf children devised by Sir Richard Paget in the 1960s. It provides an exact, grammatical signed representation of spoken English and bears no relation to traditional sign languages. Although it was intended for use with deaf children it is now mainly used with hearing children with learning disabilities.

Palantype: Palantype is a method of machine shorthand used to provide a verbatim (word-for-word) transcript of meetings either on a small visual display screen or on a full screen visible to everyone at the meeting. The operator uses a special keyboard and computer system. Reading at the same speed as speech requires good reading skills and so is normally considered to be of more use to deafened people than those who were born deaf.

Signed English (SE): A means of communication which uses signs from BSL together with finger-spelling, generated signs and grammatical markers; it is presented simultaneously with normal speech to convey exact English language patterns. It is a tool that can be used to help deaf children access features of English within an educational setting.

Sign Supported English (SSE): SSE is a manual form of communication using the same language structure as English but the manual vocabulary of BSL. In general only the word stem is signed, verb tenses etc. are omitted. It is the way in which many hearing people sign and can be understood by most deaf people, but it is not the natural language. Often people will speak while they sign thus making lip-reading possible.

Tadoma: Tadoma is a form of lip-reading by touch rather than sight used by deafblind people. The deafblind person places their thumb on the interpreter's lip and also their palm and four fingers over the speaker's throat. Helen Keller was one of the few people to use this method of receiving speech.

Teletext: Text on television. This has two uses, first there is a large amount of information written on pages of Ceefax and Oracle including special news of interest to deaf people. The second use is on page 888 on each channel which provides sub-titles for about 30 per cent of the programmes at present. This will increase to about 50 per cent over the next few years.

Textphone: Writing at a distance. A sender uses a typewriter-style keyboard and the message is transmitted by telephone line to a similar machine where the message is displayed on a screen.

Total communication: An educational system for deaf children in which all means of communication are used — signing, lip-reading, writing, drawing, videos and mime.

Typetalk: A service provided by British Telecom where one person speaks to an interpreter who transmits the message by teletext and vice versa. Used by a deaf person to communicate with a hearing person who does not own a teletext machine and vice versa.

Visual frame signing: A method of communicating with people who are deaf and have very limited sight, often tunnel vision caused by Usher Syndrome. The signer uses standard British Sign Language signs but keeps the hands within the deaf person's limited visual frame and remains a fixed distance away, normally about six feet.

Voice-over: When an interpreter provides a simultaneous translation from a sign language into a spoken language.

Advice for successful communication with people who are deafened or hard of hearing

The problem

1. The problem is not just one of volume, often clarity and distinction are also lost, so making it louder can simply increase the confusion.

2. Every hard of hearing person has a different ability to hear or communicate. It is essential to work out what is the right method of communicating for this particular individual and adapting to it.

3. Deafness is still a stigmatising condition and attitude can make all the difference. We can add to the stigma or take it away. Being friendly or relaxed, patient and gentle, will go a long way, as will making it clear we don't mind trying again and again until we get it right!

Before speaking

1. Attract attention by calling, waving or tapping on the shoulder.

2. Turn so that your full face is visible.

3. Move so that the light from the window or lamp is on your face. Lip-reading is even harder if your face is in the shadow.

4. A hearing aid will amplify background noise as well as voices. Turn off the TV or radio. Move away from other people talking and machinery, etc.

5. Try to have both your heads at the same level, either both standing or both sitting.

6. Don't get too close. The ideal distance apart is 3 to 6 feet.

When speaking

1. Make eye contact.

2. Do not speak too fast or too slow. Maintain the natural rhythm of speech.

3. Speak clearly but do not exaggerate.

4. Speak up a little but do not shout.

5. Ensure there is a clear view of your face. Do not turn away, put your hand in front of your mouth, smoke or eat. Shave off your beard from around your lips.

6. Lip-reading is only possible if both people are relaxed.

Confirming comprehension

1. The topic of the conversation must be clear at the start. Lip-reading is partly guesswork and it is a lot easier to guess a word if it is known what is being spoken about.

2. Pause at the end of each sentence to allow time to work out what has been said.

3. Think before you speak, not halfway through the sentence. Vague thoughts cannot be lip-read.

4. Write down essential information. Names, addresses and numbers are hard to lip-read accurately. Instructions and directions need to be fully understood.

5. Repeat your words if asked. The first time repeat the whole sentence or phrase. The second time repeat using different words.

Do not just repeat single words which are often difficult to understand out of context.

6. Body language, natural gestures and facial expression all help understanding.

Sign languages

1. Some deafened people understand finger-spelling. This can be learnt by young people in an evening and is a great help in communicating names.

2. For those people who prefer to use Sign Supported English or British Sign Language at interviews and meetings, please use an interpreter.

This appendix is based on the leaflet *A Few Tips for Successful Communication with Deaf People*, produced by the National Association of Deafened People and Hearing Concern.

APPENDIX C

Deaf people and the diocese

A paper approved by the Advisory Board of Ministry at their meeting in March 1996 for circulation to chaplains and diocesan committees responsible for Ministry among Deaf People.

Introduction

1.1   The Church now accepts that deaf people should not be seen as people to be looked after by Missions but as part of the Body of Christ, as members of the Church in their own right, and that they must be enabled to take a full part in the life of the Church.

1.2   However, there will remain communication difficulties. Each diocese needs to find the most appropriate structure for ministering to deaf people and for enabling them to minister within the full life of the Church.

1.3   A diocese cannot entirely hand over the spiritual care of deaf people to another organisation. Where another organisation assists in the spiritual care of deaf people, the responsibilities and structure must reflect the undivided nature of the Body of Christ.

1.4   Worship for deaf people may either be integrated into the worship of hearing people with the use of interpreters or may be sep-arate. However, it is very difficult to maintain a proper balance between the visual world of deaf people and the aural world of hearing people when all services are integrated.

1.5   The basic unit of a Church having deaf people as members is the local community meeting in a member's home, a deaf club hall or chapel, a social services hall or a parish church, with integrated or separate services.

1.6   These communities need to build their own links with the local parish or deanery for co-ordinating work in the community, shared worship and training.

1.7   In an episcopal, synodical Church every diocese will require three elements in their structure to support and nurture these communities:

(a)   A meeting of all the deaf Christians in the diocese or of deaf people representing each of the deaf congregations.

(b)   A link between the deaf people and the hearing people at diocesan level.

(c)   The ordained and lay ministry within the deaf community.

1.8   Since the number of deaf people in a diocese is relatively small and the community is dispersed, it is important, whenever possible, that the Churches of all denominations work together.

Diocesan Deaf Church Conference

2.1   In a small diocese with only one congregation of deaf people the Diocesan Deaf Church Conference will be formed in a similar way to a Parochial Church Council. In a larger diocese, representatives of each of the deaf congregations will meet together in a similar way to a Deanery Synod. All the members of the Conference are deaf, ordained or lay.

2.2.   In those dioceses where it does not already exist, it is important that the Conference is encouraged to develop its own constitution and manner of working in consultation with the National Deaf Church Conference. The responsibilities need to be agreed within the diocesan structure.

Diocesan Committee for Ministry among Deaf People

3.1   The task of this Committee is to represent the interests of the deaf people to the hearing people in the diocese and vice versa.

3.2   This Committee will in most dioceses be a sub-committee of, or will report to, the Bishop's Council, Board for Social Responsibility, or Board for Ministry. The Committee will help develop, support and monitor the ministry of the Church among Deaf People. It will co-operate with the Diocesan Deaf Church Conference in the organisation of special services, activities, events, etc.

3.3.   Membership

- In order to give the Committee strength and authority in the diocese, the leader, or chair, should be a recognised diocesan figure, a Suffragan or Archdeacon, for example. Other members should be able to offer expertise and understanding of finance, social policy and education.

- The size of the Committee will be determined by the need to balance the representatives of the Deaf Church communities and diocesan structure, but it should not be too large, but large enough to ensure a quorum of able people at all meetings.

3.4   Duties

- To consult and co-operate with the Diocesan Deaf Church Conference, to ensure that the views of deaf people are reflected in the diocesan thinking concerning the place of deaf people in Church and society and all other relevant matters.

- To ensure that diocesan policy is effectively communicated to the Deaf Church communities, and that their views are taken into account.

- To develop, support and monitor the work of the Church among Deaf People in the diocese.

- To develop and support the work of deaf people, deafened people and the hard of hearing in Church life.

3.5 Tasks

- To obtain resources for the Deaf Church communities.

- To support and monitor the work and training of the chaplains.

- To encourage and support deaf people in training for appropriate ministries.

- To promote the provision of loop and other systems in order to assist communication for deafened and hard of hearing people.

- To promote Deaf Awareness Training for Church members and especially clergy and diocesan staff.

- To inform parishes about the work of the Church among Deaf People in the diocese.

- To present regular reports to the diocese.

3.6 Working method

- Skilled interpreting must be provided for all meetings.

- All Committee members should have Deaf Awareness Training.

- Normal diocesan accounting practice should apply, i.e. with regard to budgets, forecasts and book-keeping.

- Normally the Committee should meet three to four times a year.

Ministry

4.1 In the Church working among deaf people normally there will be ordained and lay ministers, deaf or hearing.

4.2 The tradition in the Church is for ministers to complete their training before they start their authorised ministry. Regrettably, in the past and present, this has not been the case in the Church among Deaf People.

4.3   Every diocese should have an adequate number of qualified ordained chaplains to ensure that the sacramental ministry of the Church is available to every deaf person in their own language.

4.4   Every diocese should have an adequate number of qualified licensed ministers to ensure that the non-sacramental worship and pastoral ministry of the Church are available to every deaf person in their own language.

4.5   The sacramental, liturgical and pastoral ministry should not stop when a minister goes on holiday, or when there is a vacancy.

4.6   Every diocese needs a chaplain who holds the Diploma for Ministry among Deaf People and at least one other minister skilled in sign language who has time to assist when required.

4.7   The number of stipendiary chaplains required to provide an adequate standard of ministry depends on the size of the diocese, its population, the number of deaf communities, and the number of licensed lay workers.

4.8   Normally the equivalent of one full-time ordained stipendiary chaplain is required for a diocese with a population of a million people. But where the deaf communities are widely separated, it may be more appropriate to appoint an equivalent number of part-time chaplains. Nevertheless, all chaplains, whether full- or part-time, should be competent at communicating in the deaf community.

4.9   All Diocesan Committees for Ministry among Deaf People need to have regard to the future requirement for ministers, both in their own diocese and in the whole of the Church, when preparing a strategy for the allocation and training of clergy.

APPENDIX D

Chaplains: Numbers and qualifications

1.1   In April 1996 there were 48 chaplains working with deaf people
in the Church of England, all ordained priests.

Table 1   Numbers

	Full-time	Two-thirds	Half-time	One-third or one quarter	Less than 10% of full-time	Total
Qualified chaplains	10 (inc 1 NSM)	1	1	1 inc 3 NSM)	–	13
Unqualified chaplains	5	2	11	9 (inc 4 NSM)	8	35
Total	15	3	12	10	8	48

2.1

Table 2 Age structure of chaplains

Age	30–34	35–39	40–44	45–49	50–54	55–59	60–64	Total
Men	–	5	6	2	6	3	8	30
Women	1	2	5	1	6	2	1	18
Total	1	7	11	3	12	5	9	48

Communication skills

3.1   The measure of communication skills is based on the CACDP exams.

3.2   Social Services Staff specialising in work with deaf people are required to have Stage Two Signing Skills on appointment and to pass the Stage Three examination within a period of one or two years as a condition of their employment.

3.3   The Stage One Examination is taken at the end of a one year – two hours a week – course. It is only an introduction to British Sign Language.

The Stage Two intermediate examination indicates the ability to carry on a conversation.

The Stage Three advanced examination indicates fluency in the language.

Table 3 Communication skill

CACDP Level	Full-time	Two-thirds	Half-time	One-third or one quarter	Less than 10% of full-time	Total
Stage 3	4	1	1	2 (inc 2 NSM)	–	8
Stage 2	8 (inc 1 NSM)	–	1	1 (inc 1 NSM)	–	10
Stage 1	3	2	7	7 (inc 2 NSM)	4	23
No exam passed	–	–	3	–	4	7
Total	15	3	12	10	8	48

Chaplains in Training

4.1   The Chaplains in Training Programme provides the understanding of deaf people and their culture which is needed by a chaplain (see paragraphs 5.28–5.37).

Table 4 Chaplains in Training

	Full-time	Two-Thirds	Half-time	One-third or one quarter	Less than 10% of full-time	Total
Diploma	10 (inc 1 NSM)	1	1	1 (inc 1 NSM)	–	13
Intermediate	3	–	–	2 (inc 1 NSM)	–	5
Introductory	1	1	6	4 (inc 1 NSM)	3	15
None	1	1	5	3 (inc 2 NSM)	5	15
Total	15	3	12	10	8	48

Summary

5.1   At present most chaplains when appointed have little or no prior experience of the deaf community and of their language. It is to be expected that at any one time some chaplains will be only partially qualified. However, it is clear from the above tables that full-time chaplains become qualified much more quickly than those working part-time.

5.2   The average level of communication skills of part-time chaplains is, at present, a matter for concern.

APPENDIX E

Deaf Lay Ministry Training Programme

Purpose

1.1   To provide a programme conducted in sign language to help people prepare for lay ministerial tasks including:

- Pastoral Assistants

- Readers

- Other ministries required in the Church.

Reason

2.1   The number of deaf people is comparatively small and they are scattered across the whole country. No diocese or region has a large enough number of deaf people to justify running their own courses.

2.2   A course of this type depends greatly on the inter-relationship of the students and in this respect a course on a less than national level would be too small to provide this inter-student support.

2.3   In addition, no diocese has adequate experienced staff to run their own course.

Aim

3.1   To provide a flexible ministerial foundation programme, which will allow a number of levels of participation, from beginners to those undertaking Reader training. The programme will produce a more confident, committed and knowledgeable Church among Deaf People.

Method

4.1   The programme is composed of:

● regular meetings with the local chaplain;

● residential weekends;

● regional activities;

● suitable diocesan training and fellowship.

4.2   The programme is based on the life and liturgies of the deaf congregations of the Church of England, although the involvement of the other churches working among deaf people is welcomed.

Admission

5.1   Admission to the programme requires the support of the candidate's diocesan chaplain and congregation.

Chaplains

6.1   The diocesan chaplains are essential to the success of this programme. They are responsible for agreeing an appropriate personal schedule of prayer and bible reading with their candidates and for arranging and supervising training at diocesan level. They also monitor the progress of the candidates' ministry. Chaplains are supported by annual meetings of chaplains with candidates on the programme, attendance at which is considered a priority. Chaplains in training are required to attend one DLMTP weekend.

Syllabus for weekends

7.1   At each weekend there is a leader and a chaplain. There are activities that extend the student's experience of or skills in:

- personal devotional and reflective prayer;

- proclamatory activity;

- liturgical experience, and/or pastoral activity.

7.2 The syllabus for the weekends forms a rolling programme and students can start at any time.

Year One

Spring   The Easter Story – Holy Week and Resurrection.

                Knowing the story, and using it.

Summer   The Body of Christ – The Church.

                The Church of England, where do we fit in?

                Models of ministry.

Autumn   Death, dying and bereavement.

                Ministry to people who have been bereaved, and resources available.

                The Christian view of death. Funerals.

Year Two

Spring   A Worshipping People – Liturgy.

                How liturgy developed.

                Planning and leading worship.

                What is worship?

Summer   Christian service and witness to the world, the wider Church.

                Looking beyond ourselves.

Autumn   God with us – the incarnation.

                The Body of Christ today, living as a Christian.

                Christian lifestyle. Ethics, moral questions.

                How do we communicate this to the world?

Year Three

Spring   Passiontide – the Drama.

                What has the death of Jesus got to do with my life?

Summer   I believe – personal life and spiritual growth.

                Religious experience, prayer, growing in faith.

Autumn   Hard questions – the doubts which people have.

                How do we deal with uncertainties?

Spiritual development

8.1   Each candidate is guided in an appropriate personal schedule of prayer and bible reading, usually by the diocesan chaplain.

Contract

9.1   During the first six months of their training the student and their chaplain draw up a Ministerial Contract as a practical means of supporting the candidate and determining training needs.

9.2   The contract sets out an agreed area of responsibility and schedule of activity decided between the candidate and the chaplain. It is to be approved by the appropriate Diocesan Lay Ministry Officer and registered with the Secretary to CMDP.

9.3   The contract includes an agreed schedule with the diocesan chaplain for support and supervision.

9.4   All candidates keep a written record/diary of their work and experience.

Assessment

10.1   The personal assessment programme consists of:

• their own chaplain's assessment of progress;

• interviews by the programme leaders;

• written material in response to tasks set in preparation for weekends.

Certification

11.1   A certificate stating that the course has been satisfactorily completed is presented to candidates subject to:

• the approval of the diocesan chaplain;

• attendance at, at least, six out of the nine weekends in not more than three years, including satisfactory presentation of tasks set in preparation for the weekends;

• the approval of the programme leaders.

Readers

12.1   Candidates for Reader ministry must attend all nine weekends, in an extended time if necessary, and also have appropriate involvement in the fellowship and training programmes for Readers in their dioceses.

Appendix F

List of helpful addresses

Advisory Board of Ministry (ABM)
Church House
Great Smith Street
London SW1P 3NZ
Advises the House of Bishops and General Synod on all matters relating to ministry.

British Deaf Association (BDA)
1-3 Worship Street
London EC2A 2AB
An association of deaf people working to advance and protect the interests of the deaf community.

Committee for Ministry among Deaf People (CMDP)
Advisory Board of Ministry
Church House
Great Smith Street
London SW1P 3NZ
Works to develop the Church among Deaf People.

Council for the Advancement of Communication with Deaf People (CACDP)
Pelaw House
School of Education
University of Durham
Durham DH1 1TA
Works to improve all forms of communication for deaf people. See also Glossary.

Friends for Young Deaf People (FYD)

East Court Mansion Council Offices

College Lane

East Grinstead

West Sussex RH19 3LT

Encourages and enables young deaf people to develop themselves and become active members of society.

Hearing Concern

(formerly The British Association of the Hard of Hearing)

7/11 Armstrong Road

London W3 7JL

Works to assist people who are hard of hearing.

Link Centre for Deafened People (LINK)

19 Hartfield Road

Eastbourne

East Sussex BN21 2AR

Provides advice and support for adults who are deafened.

National Association of Deafened People

Longacre

Horsleys Green

High Wycombe

Buckinghamshire HP14 3UX

Association of people who are deafened working to represent their interests.

National Deafblind League

18 Rainbow Court

Paston Ridings

Peterborough

Cambridgeshire PE4 6UP

Association of people who are deafblind working to represent their interests.

National Deaf Children's Society

15 Dufferin Street

London EC1Y 8PD

Provides advice and information for parents of deaf children.

National Deaf Church Conference

Chairperson

27 Redriff Close

Maidenhead

Berks SL6 4DJ

The National Body representing deaf members of the Church of England.

Royal Association in Aid of Deaf People (RAD)

27 Old Oak Road

London W3 7HN

RAD's object is 'To promote the spiritual, social and general welfare of deaf people'. RAD provides: advocacy, chaplaincy, counselling, information, interpreting, leisure facilities and support groups. RAD offers chaplaincy provision in association with five dioceses in South East England.

Royal National Institute for Deaf People (RNID)

19-23 Featherstone Street

London EC1Y 8SL

Provides information, interpreters and residential care for deaf people.

SENSE

The National Deafblind and Rubella Association

11/13 Clifton Terrace

Finsbury Park

London N4 3SR

Provides advice, support, information and services for deafblind children and their families.

Bibliography

Ashley, J. *Journey into Silence*, The Bodley Head: London, 1973.
   (*Autobiography of a deafened Member of Parliament.*)

Beaver, P. *A Tower of Strength: Two Hundred Years of the Royal School for Deaf Children, Margate*, The Book Guild Ltd: Lewes, 1992.

CACDP *Directory 1996/7* CACDP: Durham, 1996.
   (*Contains a list of all registered and trainee interpreters.*)

Chubb, R. *Lifting Holy Hands*, ABM Paper No 7. June 1994.
   (*A description of liturgical signs.*)

Corfmat, P. *Please Sign Here*, Churchman Publishing: Worthing, 1990.
   (*Autobiography of a chaplain and social worker.*)

Dimmock, A. F. *Cruel Legacy*, Scottish Workshop Publications: Edinburgh, 1993.
   (*An introduction to the record of Deaf People in History.*)

Grant, B. (ed.) *The Quiet Ear*, Andre Deutsch: London, 1987.
   (*Deafness in literature: an anthology*)

Gregory, S. and Hartley, G. M. (eds) *Constructing Deafness*, Open University Press: Milton Keynes, 1991.
   (*A range of different perspectives on deafness challenging established ideas.*)

Higgins, P. C. *Outsiders in a Hearing World*, Sage Books: California, 1980.

Levine, E. S. *Psychology of Deafness*, Columbia University Press: New York, 1960.

Lysons, K. *Hearing Impairment*, Woodhead Faulkner: Cambridge, 1984.

RNID Information Directory 1994/5 RNID: London, 1994.
(*Contains the addresses of all organisations, services and educational establishments for deaf people.*)

Taylor, G. and Bishop, J. (eds) *Being Deaf*, Open University Press: Milton Keynes, 1991.

   (*A description of the experience of deafness.*)

Weir, M. 'A deaf theological perspective', in *Made Deaf in God's Image*, Visible Communications: Northampton, 1996.